Draw

PATTERNS

Anna Brockett

ADAM & CHARLES BLACK · LONDON

First published 1981
A & C Black (Publishers) Ltd
35 Bedford Row, London WC1R 4JH

ISBN 0 7136 2188 5

Printed and bound in the USA at Whitehall Company, Wheeling, Il.

Contents

Making a start

For thousands of years people have made patterns, from the most primitive design scratched on to clay pots to the intricacies of Arabic tracery or contemporary op-art.

To draw patterns you don't have to be an accomplished artist—but observation of the world around you and plenty of practice in general drawing will help you to develop your ideas. The act of drawing and experimenting creates its own excitement, and you will find that the possibilities for imaginative pattern drawing are limitless.

Carry a sketchbook with you whenever possible. Make notes of shapes and ideas to be developed later, or more careful drawings of objects that can be used for reference. Look around you—at buildings, nature, people, everyday objects in the home. Ideas can be found everywhere.

The best equipment will not itself make you a better artist. But good equipment is encouraging and pleasant to use, so buy the best you can afford and don't be afraid to use it freely.

Be as bold as you dare. It's your piece of paper and you can do what you like with it. Experiment with the biggest piece of paper and the boldest, softest piece of chalk or crayon you can find, filling the paper with lines, doodles, shapes, colours, to get a feeling of freedom. You may be surprised at the ideas that will emerge.

Be self-critical. If an experimental drawing doesn't work, scrap it and start again. A second, third or even fourth attempt will often be better than the first, because you are finding out about the possibilities of your idea all the time.

Experiment with colour. Use coloured chalks, felt-tip pens or cut-up coloured paper from magazines etc., and try different arrangements of contrasting colours or shades of the same colour.

You can learn a lot about pattern from books and museums. Look for examples on pottery, oriental carpets, stained glass, tiles, fabrics, mosaics, from all periods and all parts of the world.

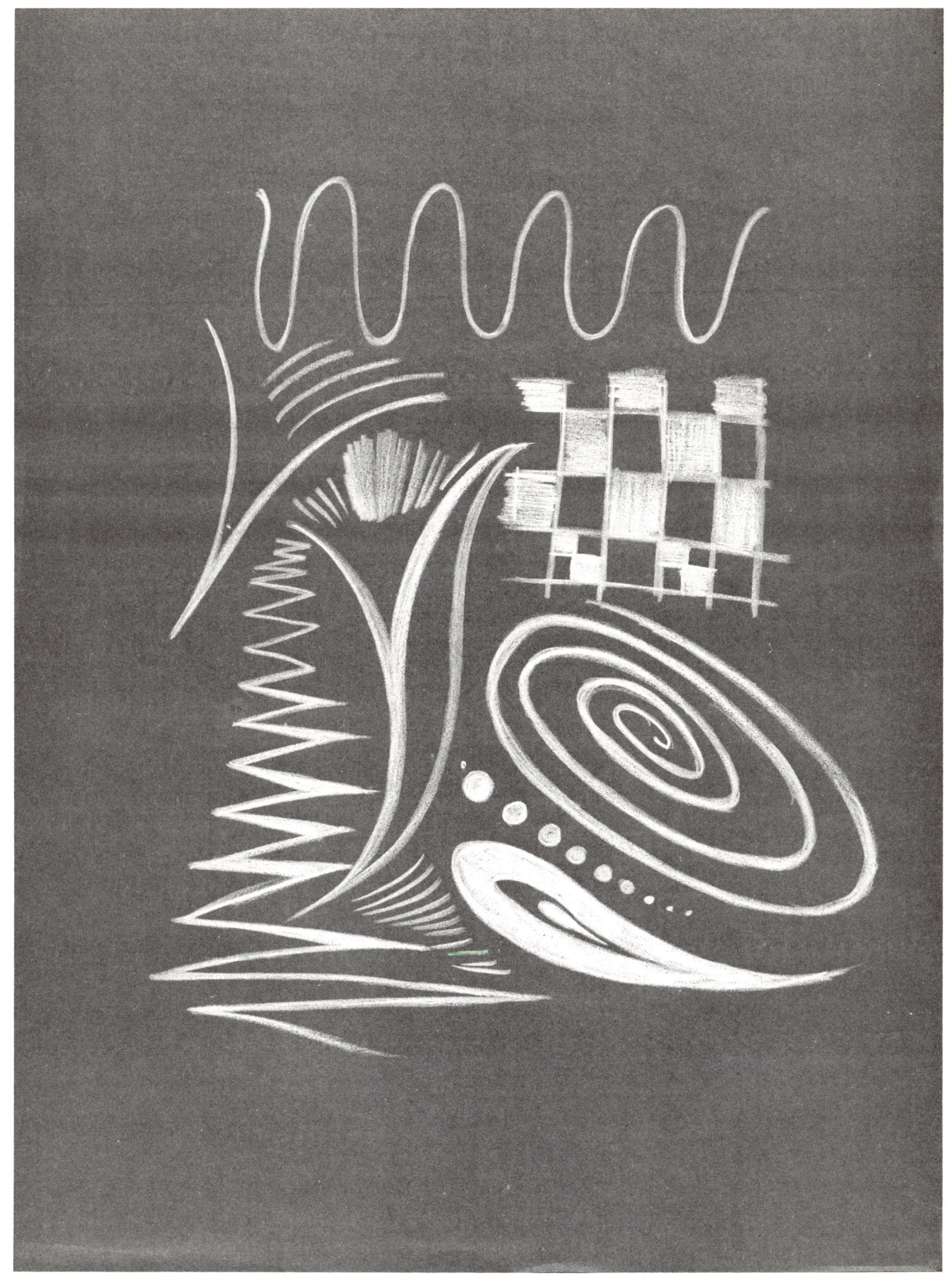

What to draw with

You will need ordinary drawing materials for making notes and collecting information, but a wider range of media and instruments will be needed for finished patterns.

Pencils are graded according to hardness, from 6H (the hardest) through 5H, 4H, 3H, 2H to H; then HB; then B, through 1B, 2B, 3B, 4B, 5B to 6B (the softest). For sketching ideas, HB or softer is best; for drawing accurate, fine lines use a harder pencil and keep it very sharp. Royal Sovereign is a fine range of graphite drawing pencils.

Charcoal (very soft) is excellent for large, bold sketches, but not for detail. To prevent smudging, spray with fixative.

Felt-tip or fibre-tip pens are good to work with, both for drawing and filling in patterns. There are broad-tipped 'markers' or finer varieties in a wide range of colours. Try 'Stabilo' markers.

Coloured crayons such as Caran d'Ache also come in a wide range of colours and can be used to fill in your patterns.

Pens vary as much as pencils or crayons.
Mapping pens are only suitable for fine work and delicate detail.

Special artists' pens, such as Gillott 303 and Gillott 404, allow you a more varied line, according to the angle at which you hold them and the pressure you use. The Gillott 659 is a very popular crowquill pen.

Reed, bamboo and quill pens are good for bold lines and you can make the nib end narrower or wider with the help of a sharp knife or razor blade. This kind of pen has to be dipped frequently into the ink.

Fountain pens have a softer touch then dip-in pens, and many artists prefer them. The portability of the fountain pen makes it a very useful sketching tool.

Special fountain pens, such as Rapidograph and Rotring, control the flow of ink by means of a needle valve in a fine tube (the nib). Nibs are available in several grades of fineness and are inter-changeable. Their main advantage is that they produce a very accurate black or coloured line for tracing a pattern. They can also be used for drawing on glass and plastic.

Inks also vary. Waterproof Indian ink quickly clogs the pen. Pelikan Fount India, which is nearly as black, flows more smoothly and does not leave a varnishy deposit on the pen. Ordinary fountain-pen or writing inks (black, blue, green or brown) are less opaque, so give more variety of tone. You can mix water with any ink in order to make it thinner. But if you are using Indian ink, add distilled or rain water, because ordinary water will cause it to curdle.

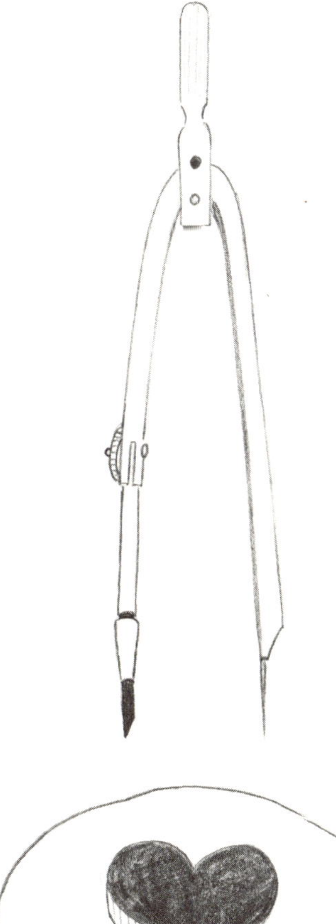

Ball point pens are cheap and fool-proof and useful for quick notes and exploratory scribbles.

Brushes are very versatile drawing instruments. The biggest sable brush has a fine point, and the smallest brush laid on its side provides a line broader than the broadest nib. To develop a steady hand with a brush, practise painting on paper before transferring patterns onto three-dimensional surfaces.

Other equipment

A good ruler with a firm edge and clear markings, and a pair of compasses, are essential items of equipment for geometric patterns. For a large repeating pattern, a T-square will help you to draw accurate guide-lines.

Potato blocks, lino blocks and stencils can all be used for applying pattern.

To make a simple potato block, cut the potato in half, then cut away the flat surface to leave the shape you want to print.

To make a stencil, trace the motif onto stencil paper and cut it out with a sharp knife. Leave a good margin round the design. Apply colour with a stencil brush or use a felt tip pen.

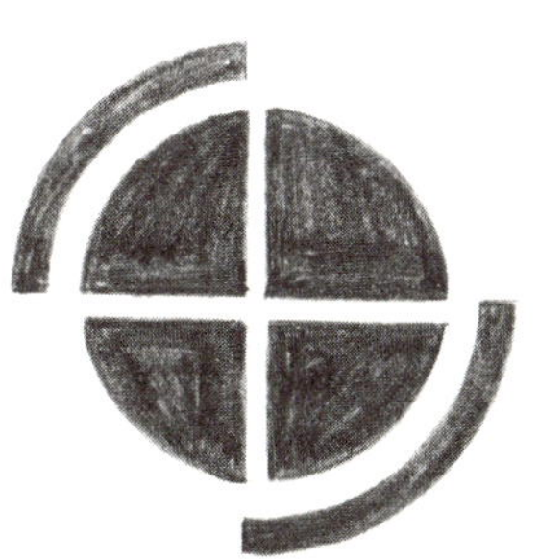

What to draw on

Try as many different surfaces as possible.

Ordinary, inexpensive paper is often as good as anything else, especially for preliminary drawing and experiment: for example, brown and buff wrapping paper (Kraft paper) and lining for wallpaper have surfaces which are particularly suitable for charcoal and soft crayons. Some writing and duplicating papers are best for pen drawings. But there are many papers and brands made specially for the artist.

Ledger Bond paper (cartridge in the UK), the most usual drawing paper, is available in a variety of surfaces—smooth, 'not surface' (semi-rough), rough.

Watercolour papers also come in various grades of smoothness. They are thick, high-quality papers, expensive but pleasant to use, and good if you want to turn your patterns into pictures, using watercolour inks.

Graph paper is ideal for geometric patterns and for working out complicated repeating patterns.

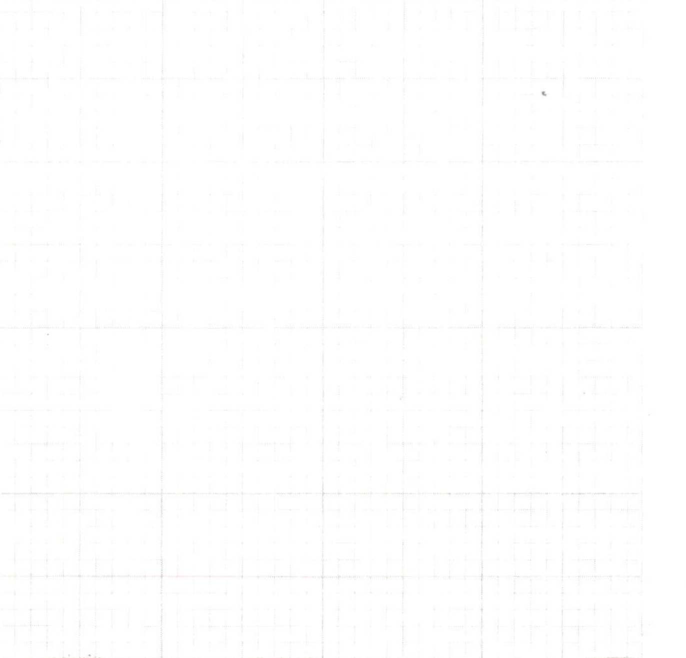

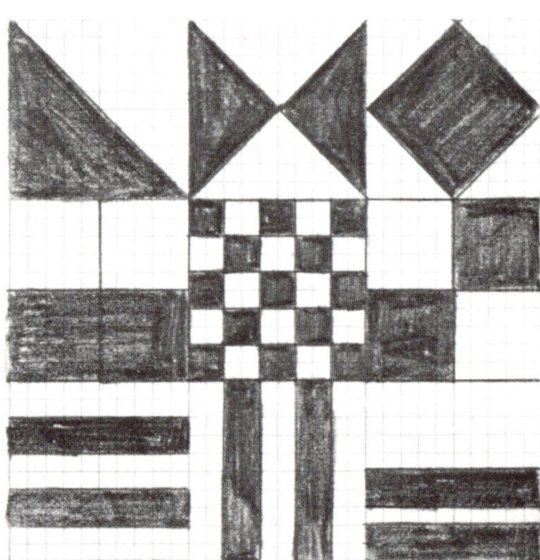

Sketchbooks, made up from nearly all these papers, are available. Choose one with thin, smooth paper to begin with. Thin paper means more pages, and a smooth surface is best to record detail.

Lay-out pads make useful sketchbooks. Although their covers are not stiff, you can easily insert a stiff piece of card to act as firm backing to your drawing. The paper is semi-transparent, but this can be useful—almost as tracing paper—especially if you are making a layout for a large pattern.

Tracing paper can also be bought in pads.

An improvised sketchbook can be just as good as a bought one—or better. Find two pieces of thick card, sandwich a stack of paper, preferably of different kinds, between them and clip together at either end.

If you are working on a large sheet of paper, it is helpful to have a drawing board to which you can pin or clip the paper. This is an expensive item to buy, but you may be able to find an unwanted piece of wood that you can cut to manageable size. The surface must be smooth, even and free from cracks.

For freehand drawing it is easier to work on a slightly tilted surface; but for measuring out a large area, or transferring a repeating pattern, you will need a flat surface.

For measuring and drawing on very large areas, you will need a table top to work on. If the surface is not completely smooth you could cover it with a sheet of hardboard, smooth side up.

Perspective

It isn't necessary to understand the laws of perspective in order to draw patterns. But sometimes perspective can create interesting patterns, so it may help to consider it briefly here.

The further away an object is, the smaller it seems.

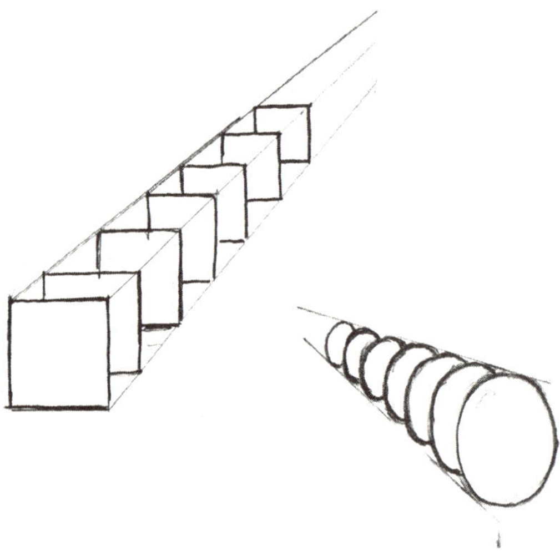

All parallel horizontal lines that are directly opposite you, at right-angles to your line of vision, remain parallel.

All horizontal lines that are in fact parallel but go away from you will appear to converge at eye-level at the same vanishing point on the horizon. Lines that are above your eye-level will seem to run downwards towards the vanishing point; lines that are below your eye-level will run upwards.

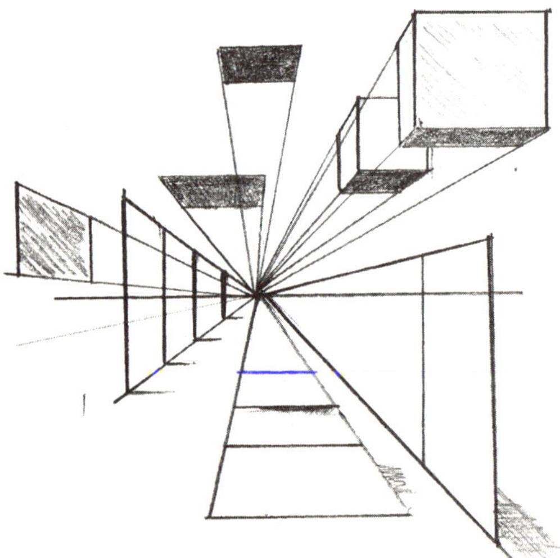

The larger and closer any object is, the bigger the front of it will seem to be in relation to the part furthest away, or to any other more distant object. Its actual shape will appear foreshortened or distorted.

Diagonal lines drawn between the opposite angles of a square or rectangle will meet at a point which is half-way along its length or breadth. This remains true when the square or rectangle is foreshortened.

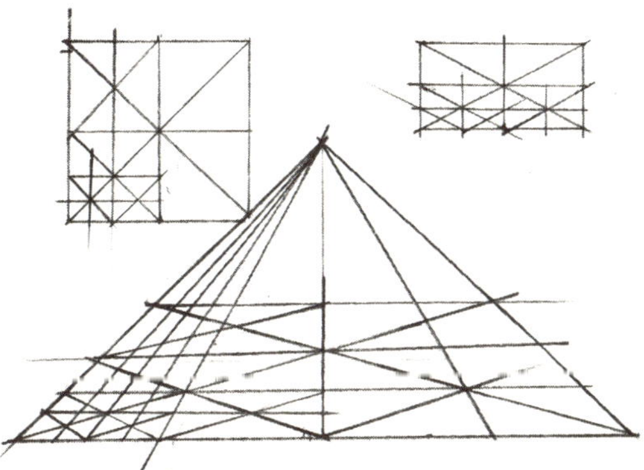

When drawing a circular shape, the following is useful: a circle drawn inside a square will touch the square at the centre point of each of its sides. A foreshortened circle will turn into an oval, but will still touch the centre points of each side of a similarly foreshortened square. However distorted the square, the circle will remain a true oval but will seem to tilt as the square moves to left or right of the vanishing point.

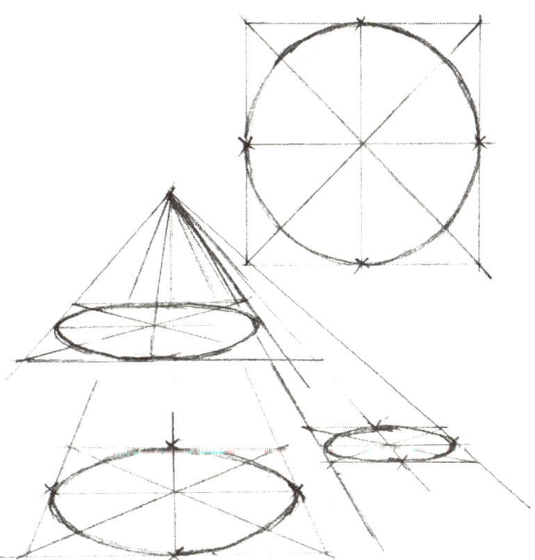

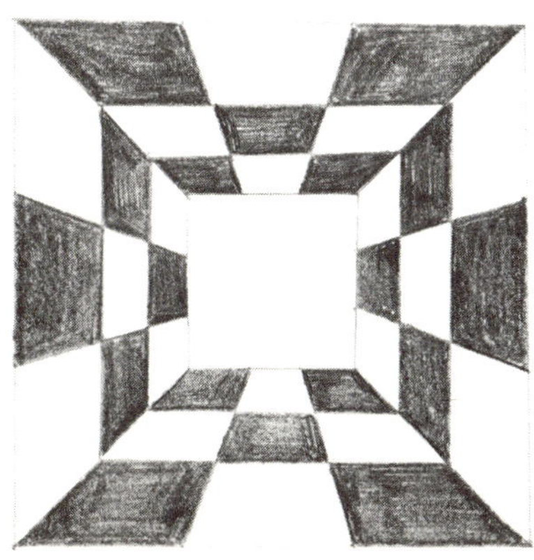

You may be able to use some of these 'rules' deliberately to create a pattern; or you may find that an effect of perspective is created incidentally by the arrangement of lines or areas of tone in a pattern, as in this drawing.

Composition

The success of even the simplest pattern depends on the placing of its elements in relation to each other and to the space they are to fill.

Before you begin drawing, think about how you will arrange your pattern on the paper and how it will grow. Decide whether you want to fill a specific space or simply let the pattern go on growing, and whether you will start from the centre or from one side.

Before starting an elaborate pattern, do some rough sketches of the main shapes to help you decide on the final composition. Alternating, repeating, enlarging and diminishing patterns all create varying and interesting effects.

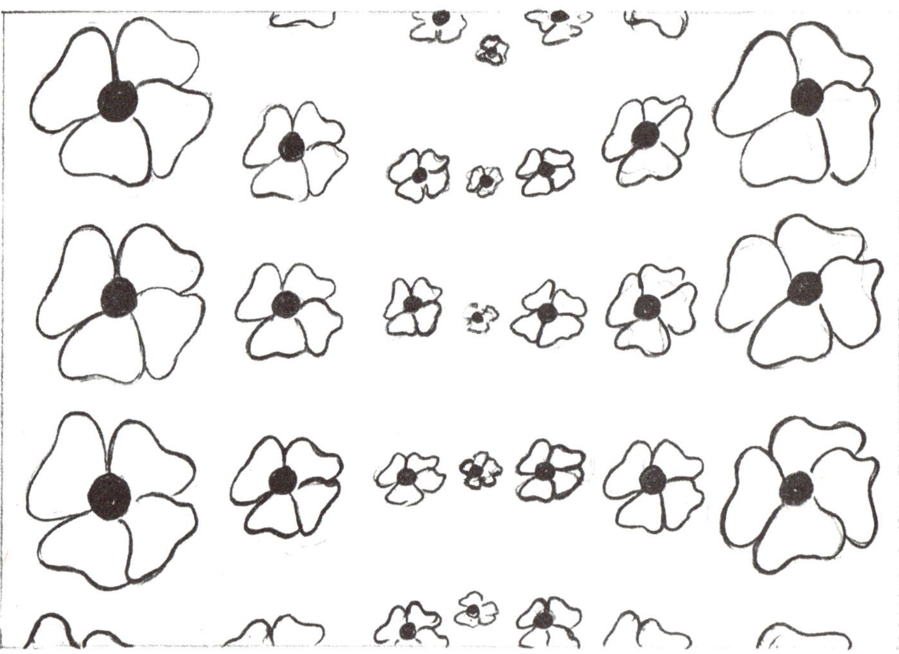

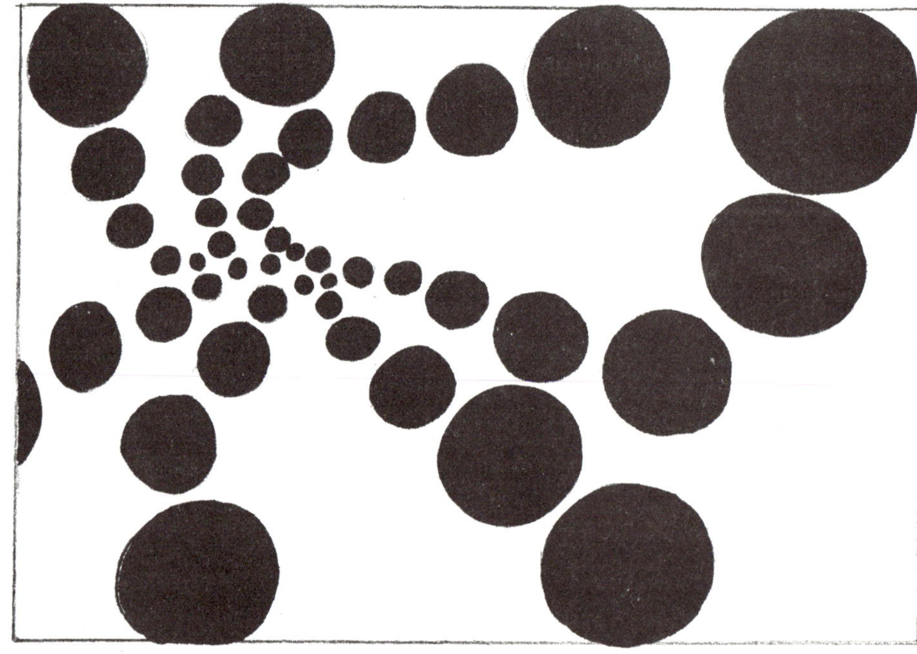

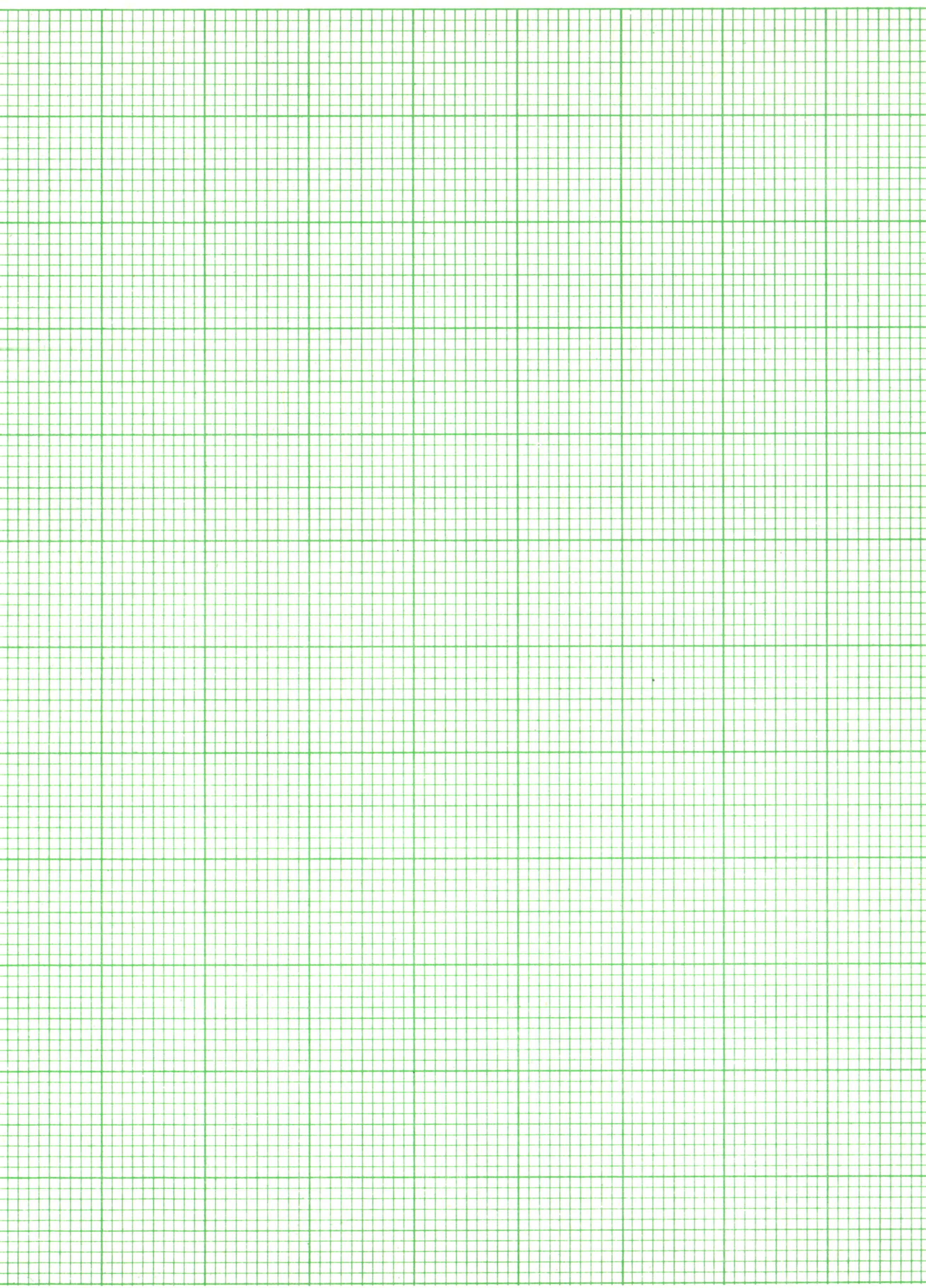

When designing a pattern to fill a specific shape, try to relate the elements and proportions of the pattern to this shape. In a repeating pattern, the placing of each motif is important. Try as many variations as possible.

Negative spaces (i.e. blank spaces) are as important as the elements of the pattern which create those spaces. Look at any regular pattern and observe how other patterns emerge from the blank spaces it creates. Here are two very simple examples.

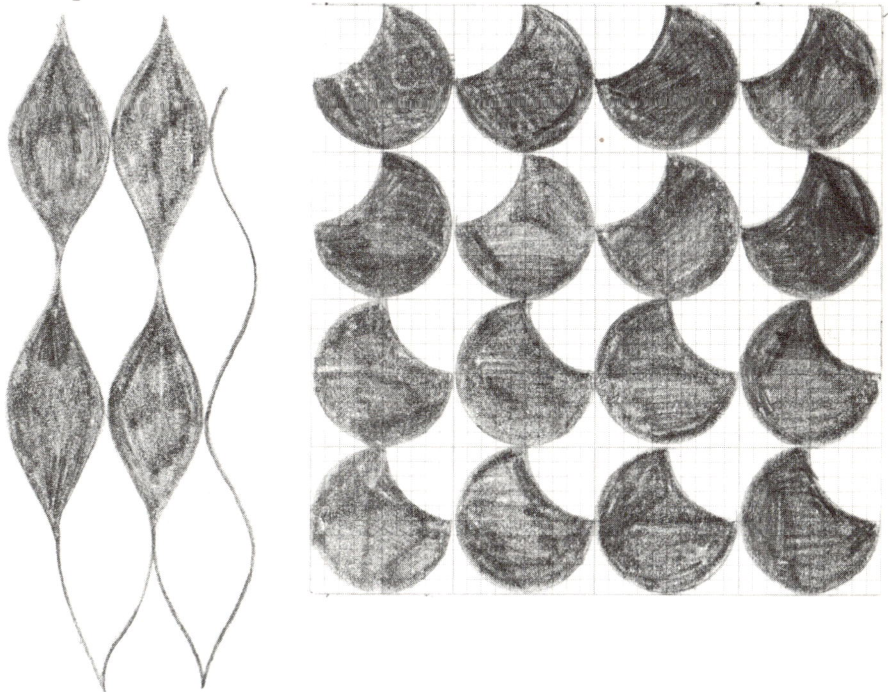

Remember, though, that rules are made to be broken. Every good artist is a good artist at least partly because of his originality, so allow you imagination to work freely. Your drawing is an expression of your individuality.

Free-style patterns

Free-style patterns can be evolved from the simplest beginnings.

Start with a page of random dots; link them with a fine line and then colour in the resulting shapes, using felt-tip pens or bright crayons.

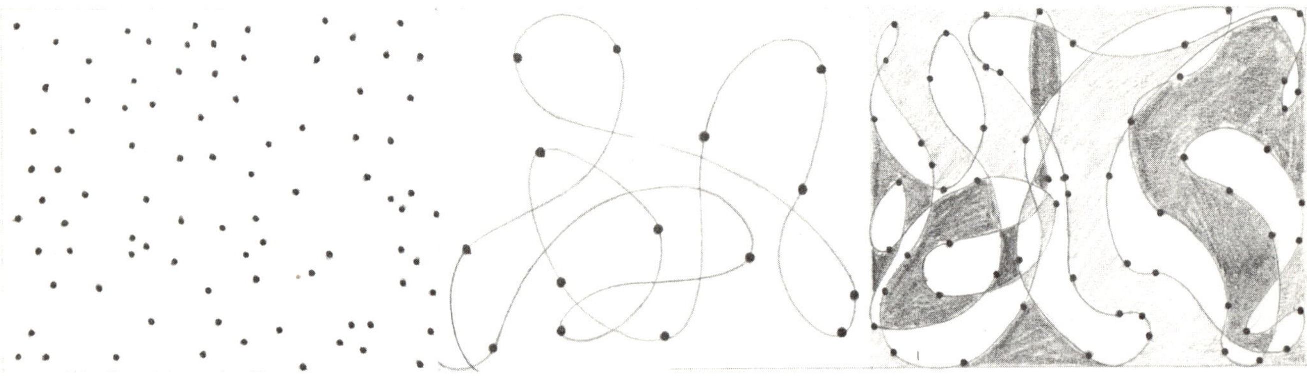

Add horizontal, vertical and diagonal lines for a more complex pattern; or fill some areas with solid colour and others with broken colour or texture.

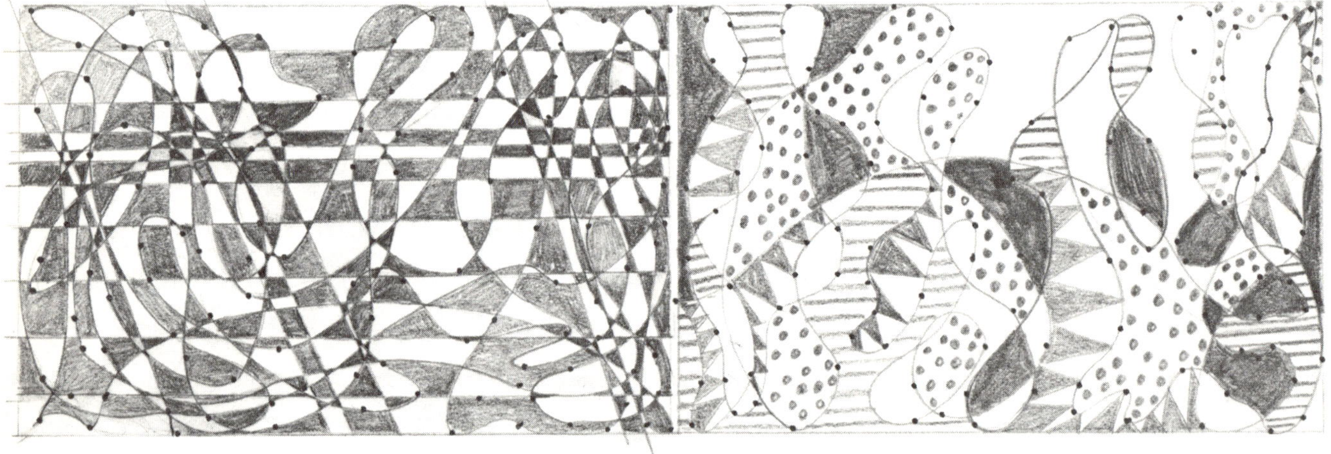

Here are some examples of a more precise, geometric kind of doodling, using compasses and a ruler and then combining these lines with free-style wavy lines. Continue to experiment with different ways of using colour.

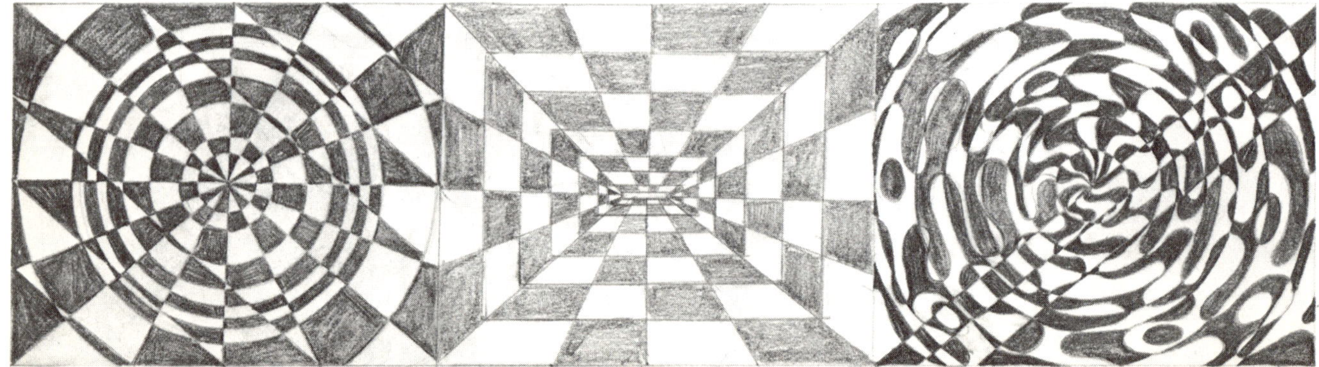

For this kind of free-style pattern, choose a shape and build up your pattern by repeating it freehand, adding colour or pattern within the shapes.

These examples each use one basic shape. Be inventive: try combining two or three shapes.

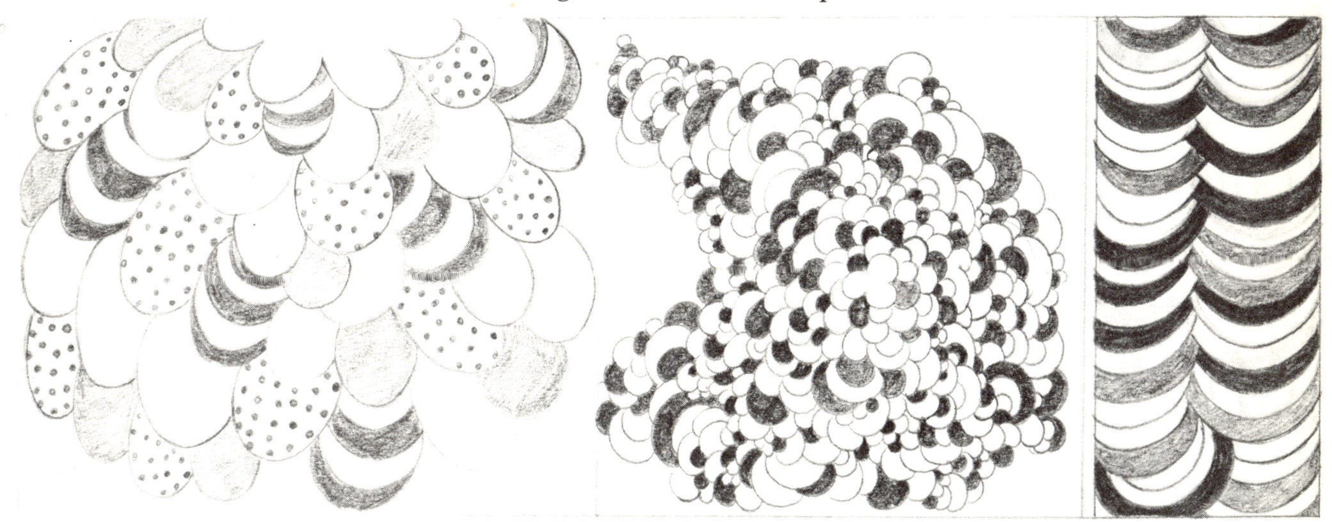

Instead of using shapes, see what can be done with simple marks, repeated either at random or in a more organised design.

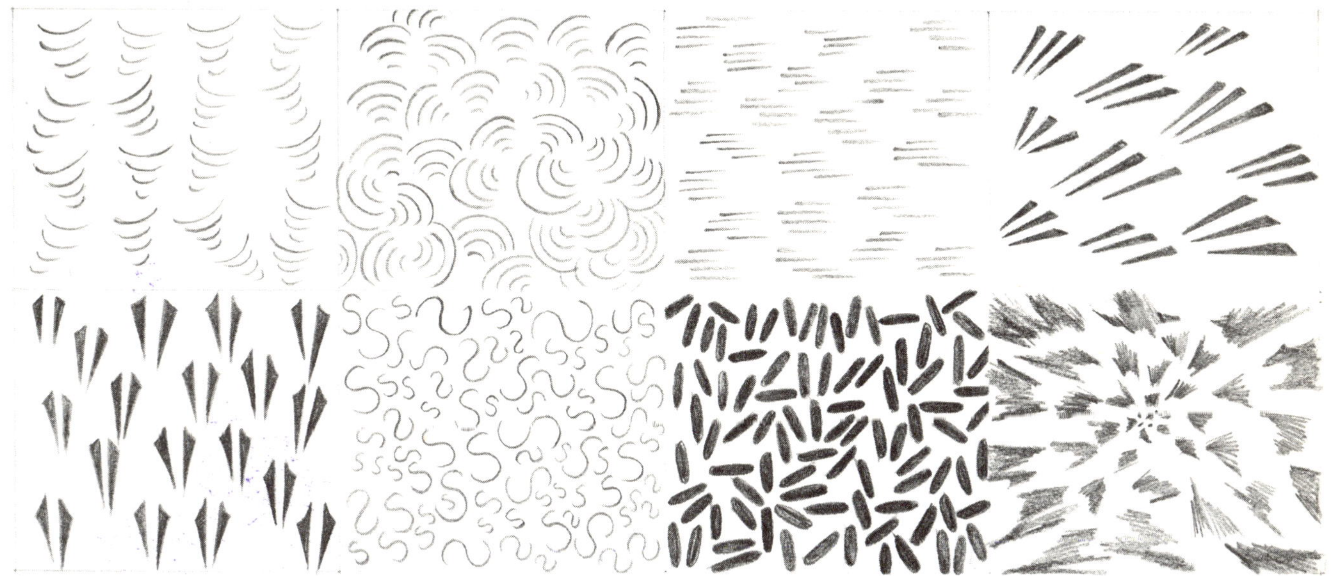

In the course of exploring these free-style patterns you may find an idea which is worth developing in a more accurate or disciplined way.

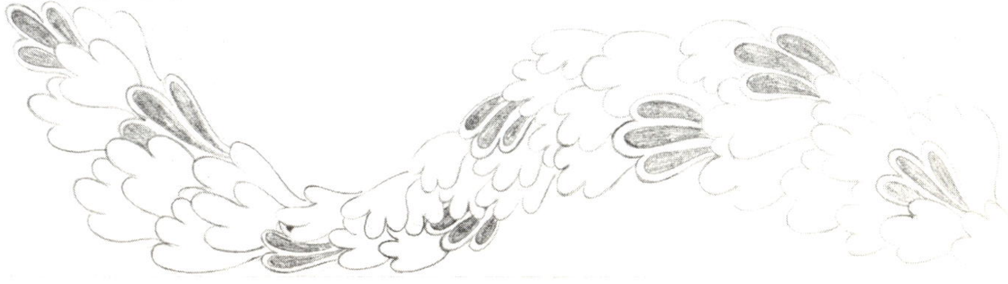

Using graph paper

Geometric patterns can be worked out accurately on graph paper, using the lines and squares as a guide and dividing them up in any way you choose.

Start by taking a basic element such as a zig-zag. From this you can build up a variety of patterns—by adding more lines, filling in different areas, using different colour combinations or contrasting areas of black and white, and by adding one line of pattern to another. This particular type of design was widely used by the Navajo Indians on their rugs.

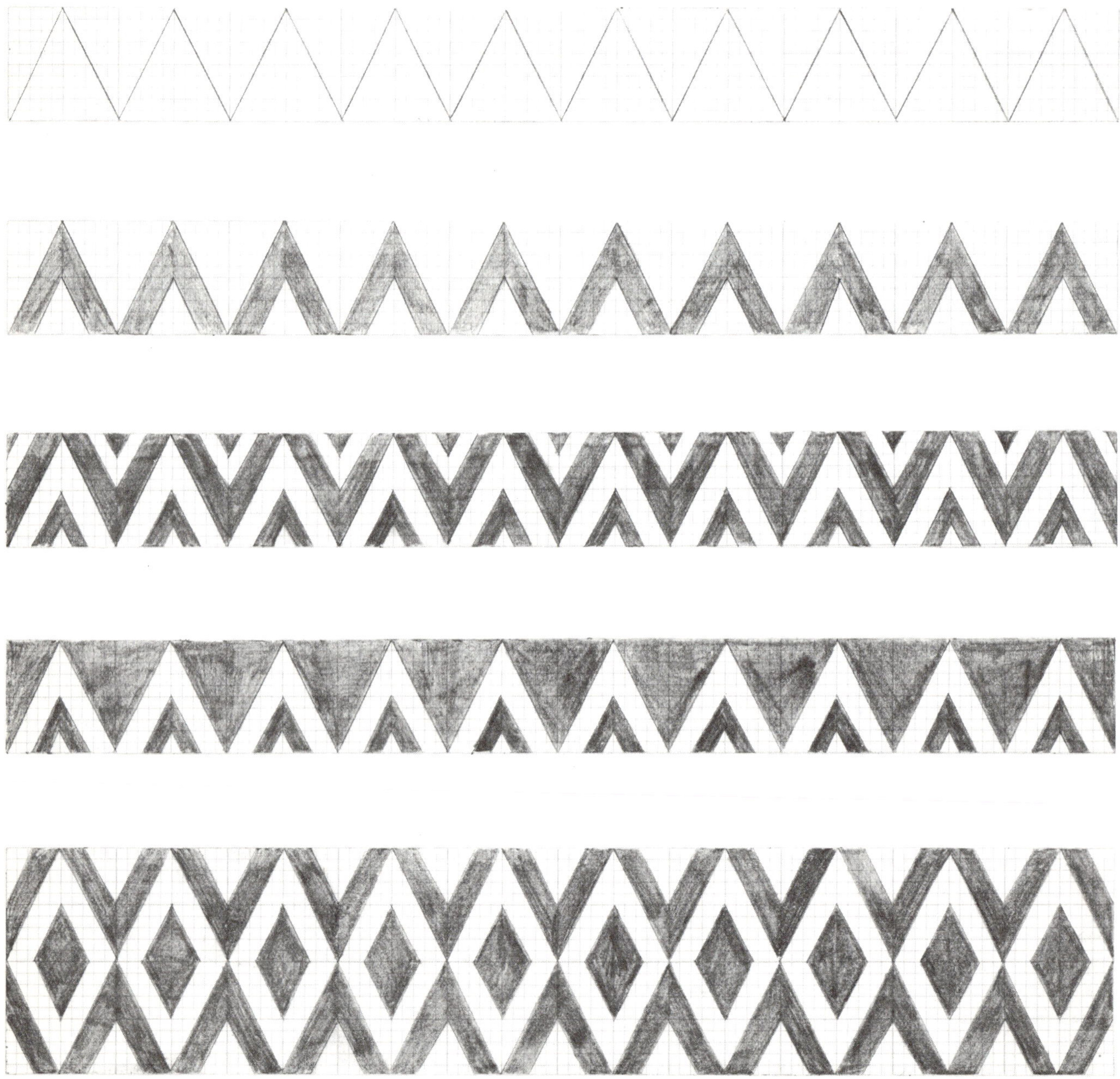

Simple patterns can be made by blocking in squares or rectangles.

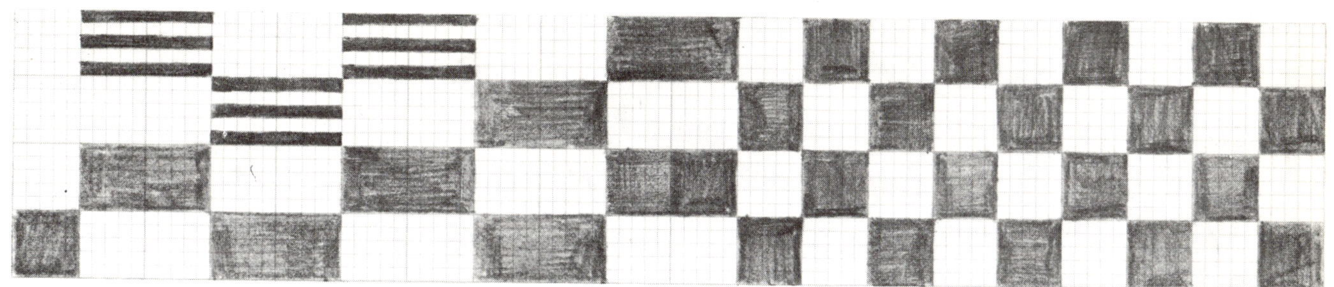

These four patterns are based on the hexagon. By filling in different parts of the basic shape you can create new shapes and motifs. See how many variations you can develop from one basic shape.

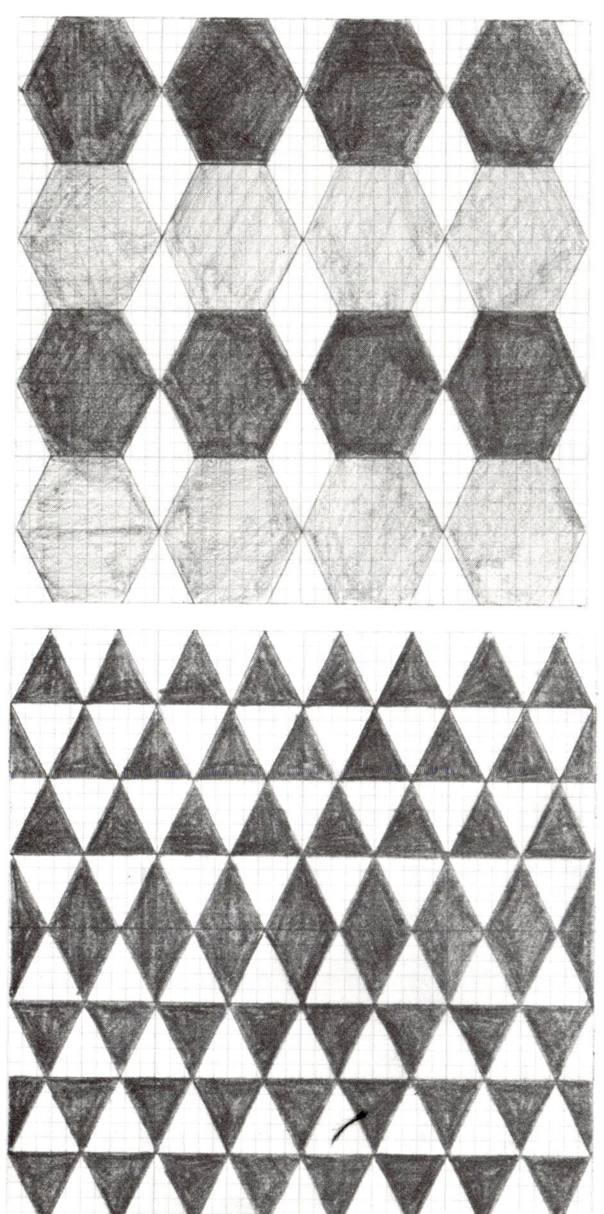

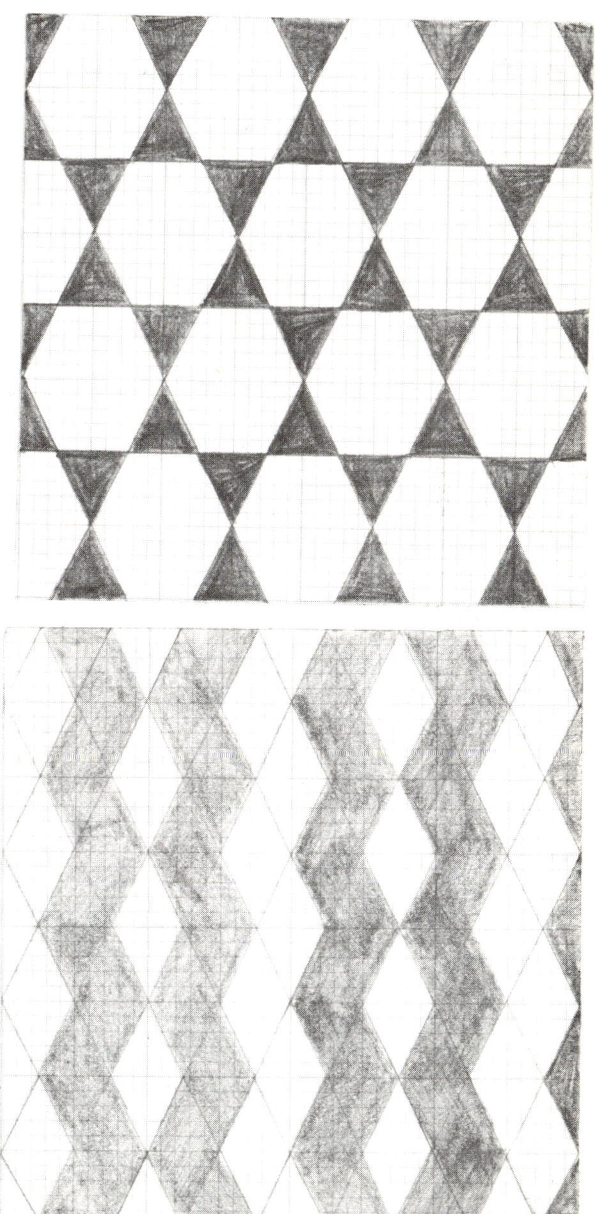

Repeating patterns

A simple repeating pattern can be made from one or two basic motifs based on a square. Here are some rough sketches which explore this idea. Keep the motif simple, and experiment with various ways of repeating it.

Instead of aligning the squares exactly, alternate rows can be dropped by half the unit height to vary the combination, as shown below, left. Or two motifs can be combined at random to build up a pattern (below, right).

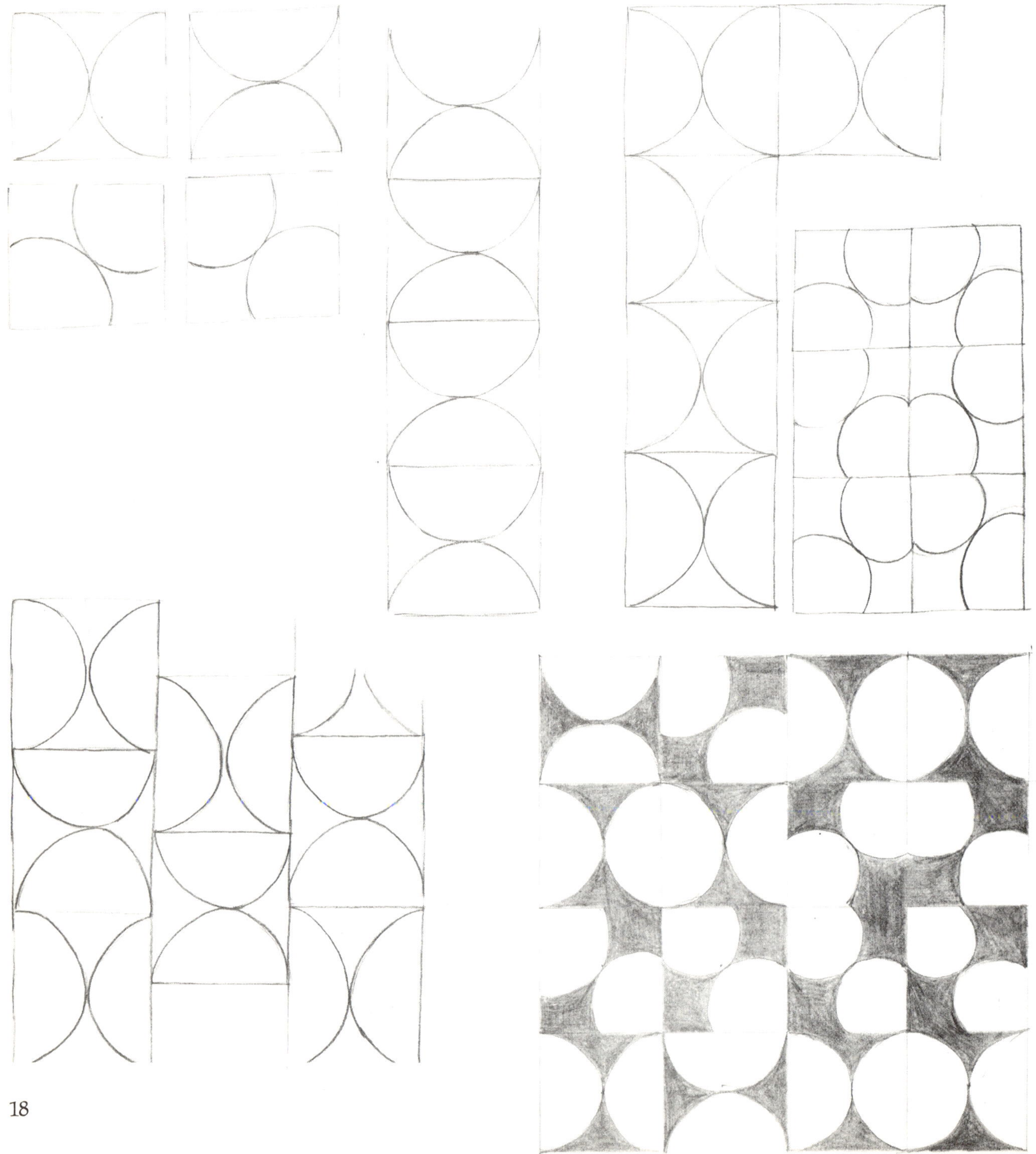

Another idea for a repeating pattern made up of identical square units. Mark a point in exactly the same position on each side of the square, and design your motif so that a line meets the edge of the square at each of these points. When placed side by side these units will always 'match'. In examples 1–4, the first square is static, the second is turned or reversed. This gives endless possibilities for variation.

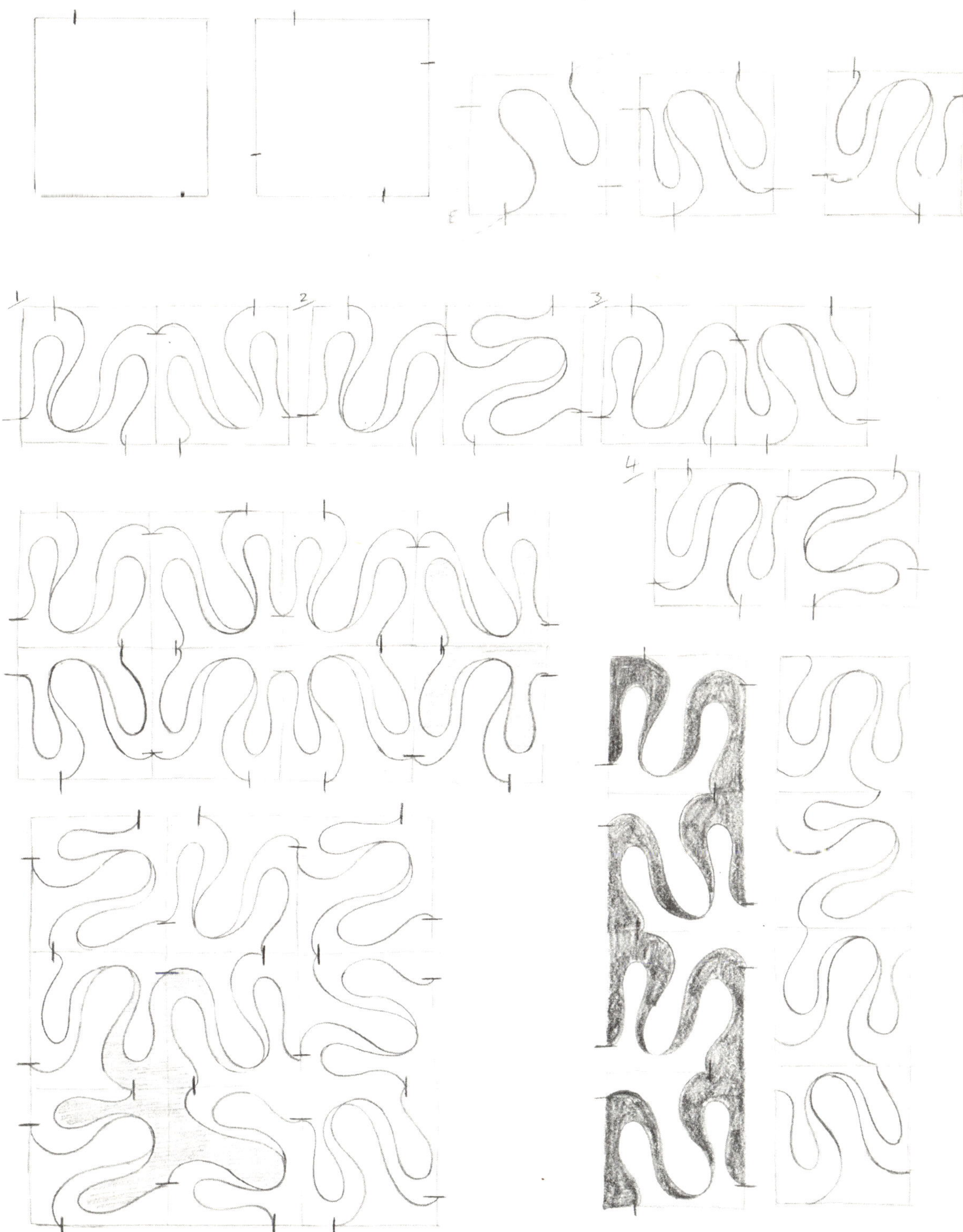

This series of patterns shows how the repetition of shapes in varying positions and combinations can be worked out accurately on graph paper.

Circles and semi-circles can be drawn with compasses, using the squares of the paper as a guide. Experiment with different arrangements and then vary the pattern by filling in the shapes with colour. Try different colour combinations, or tones of one colour, or simply black and white.

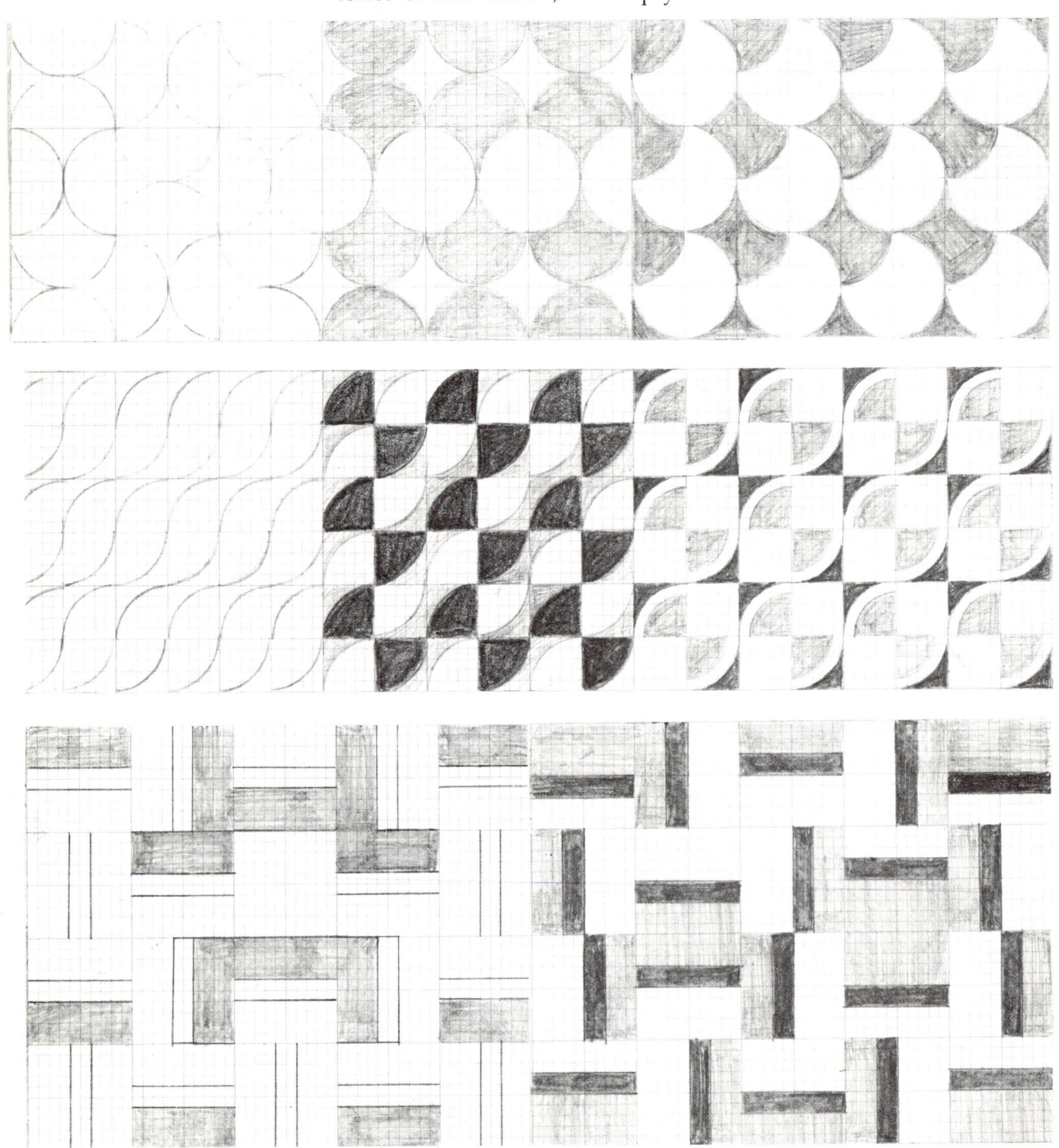

Make linear patterns by blocking in oblong shapes on the graph paper.

This group is based on diagonals. Start with a simple pattern, then vary it in as many ways as possible by the use of blocking-in and colour.

You will find that quite complicated patterns can be evolved in this way from a simple basic grid.

Try combinations of circles and oblongs, or circles and diagonals; or be more adventurous and combine all three.

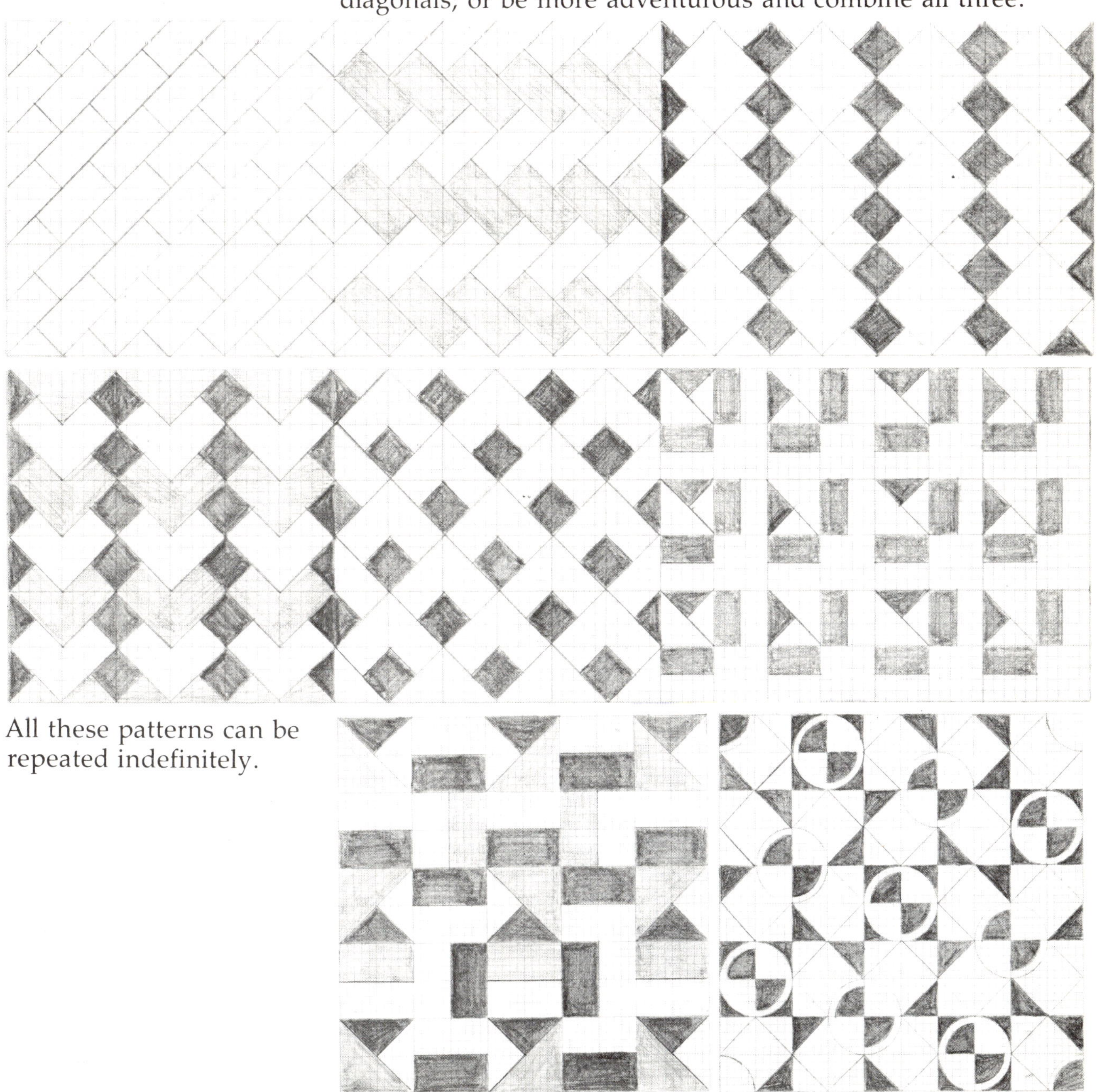

All these patterns can be repeated indefinitely.

These examples combine all the basic elements shown on the previous pages—squares, circles, rectangles, diamonds and triangles.

The first pattern shows how the blank area defined by the motif can be as important as the motif itself.

I have used felt-tip pens here to give the patterns a more finished appearance.

The page opposite shows what can happen when you work on a larger scale and allow your imagination to flourish.

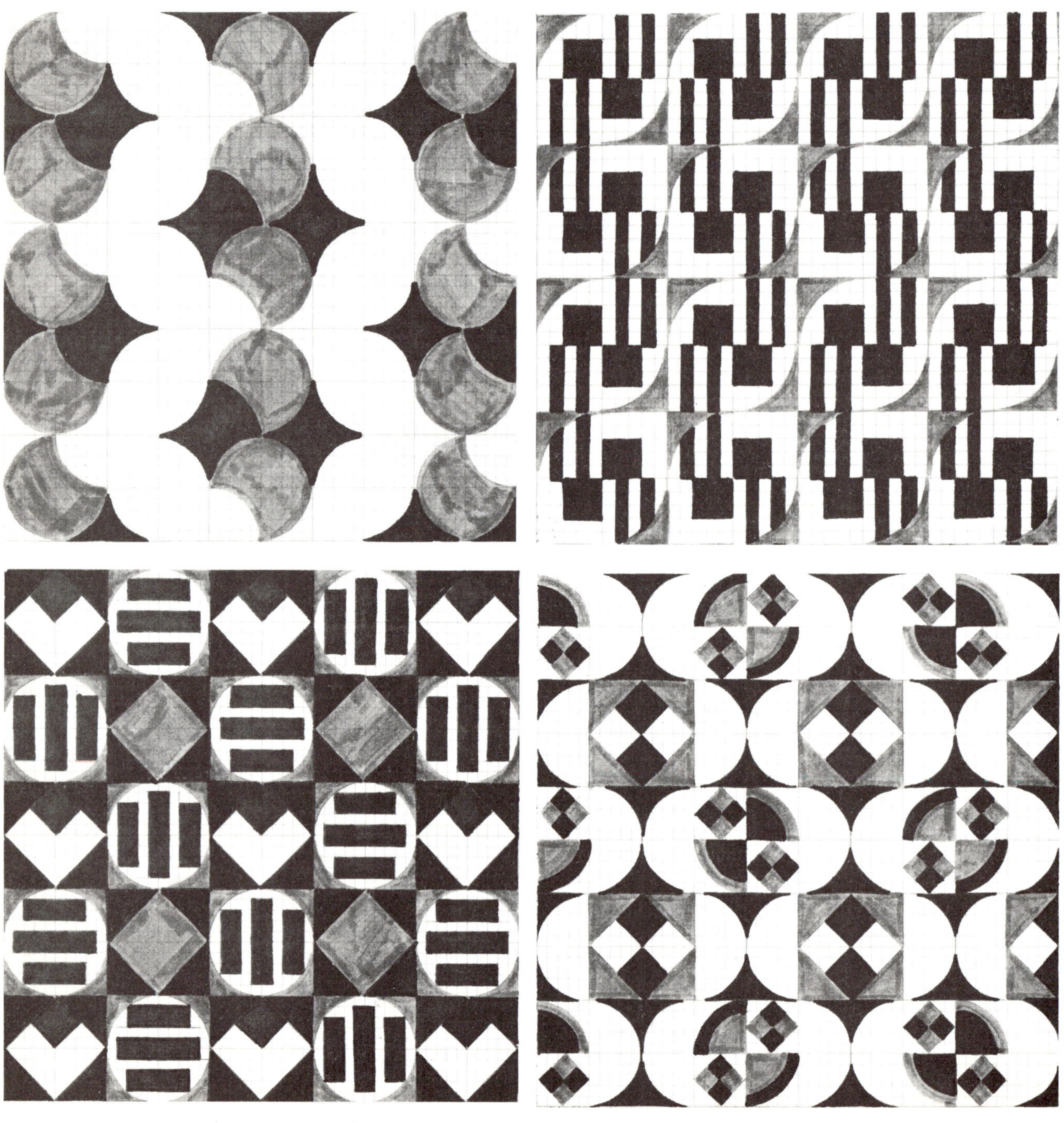

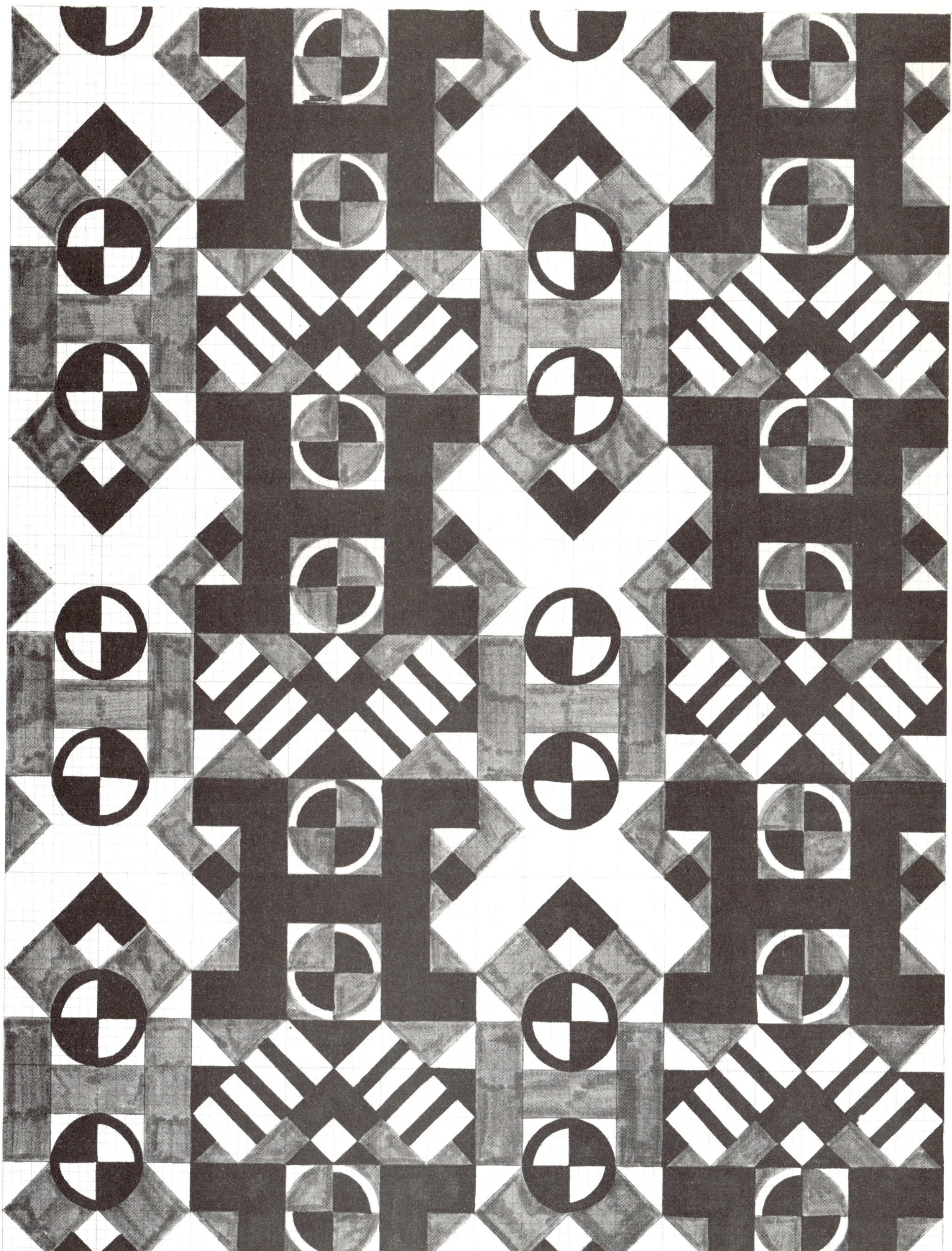

Here are some ideas for repeating patterns using free-hand motifs, that could be used, for example, on textiles or wrapping paper.

Divide your paper accurately into squares or diamonds with a lightly-drawn pencil line, using a T-square to get the lines parallel. Choose a simple motif that is easy to draw, and start to build up your pattern, using the grid as a guide.

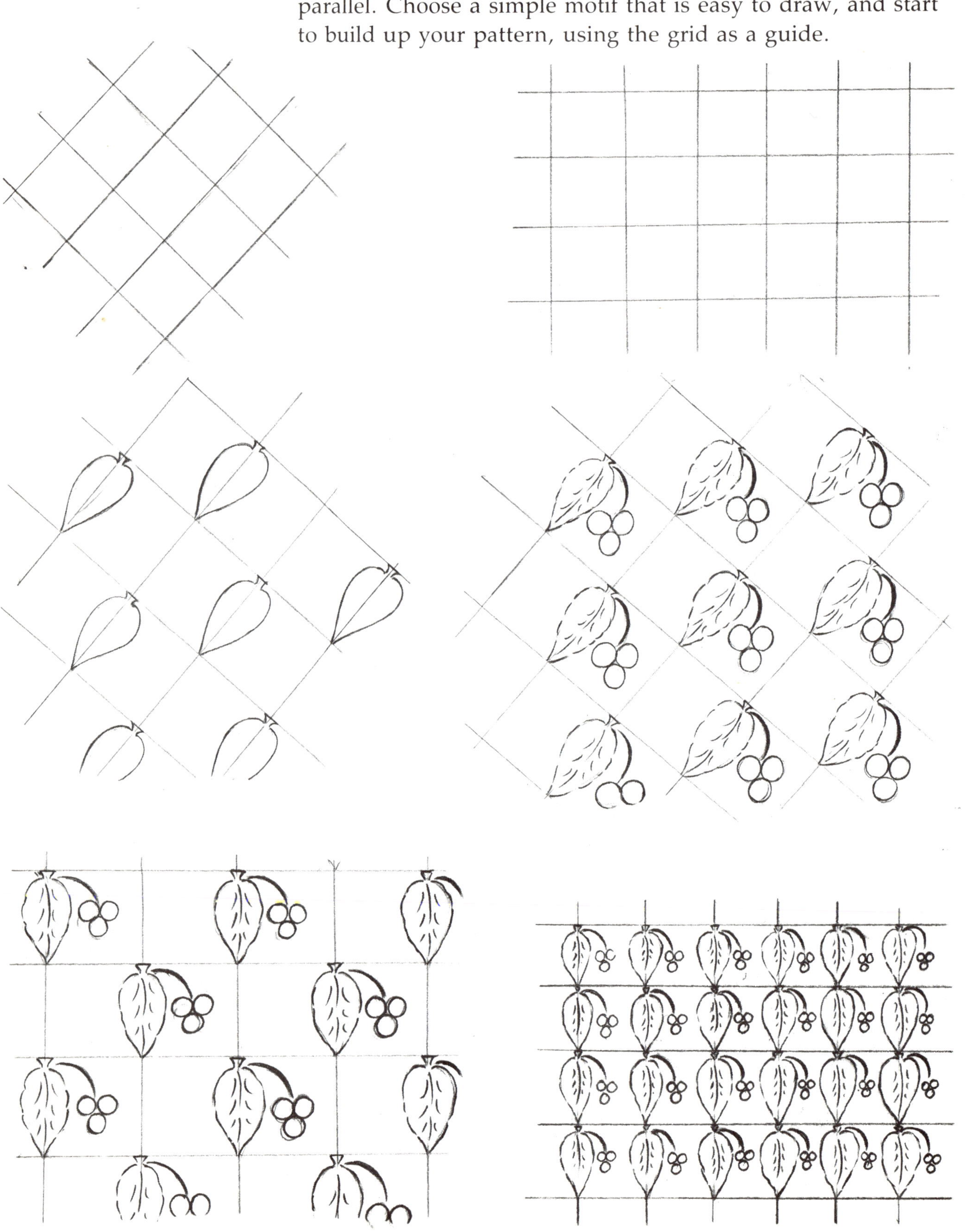

Experiment with different arrangements of the same motif. Then try combining two motifs, or even three. You can vary the effect by drawing the pattern on coloured paper.

You may find it easier to trace the motif. Even with guide-lines, it can be quite difficult to draw the same shape repeatedly over a large area.

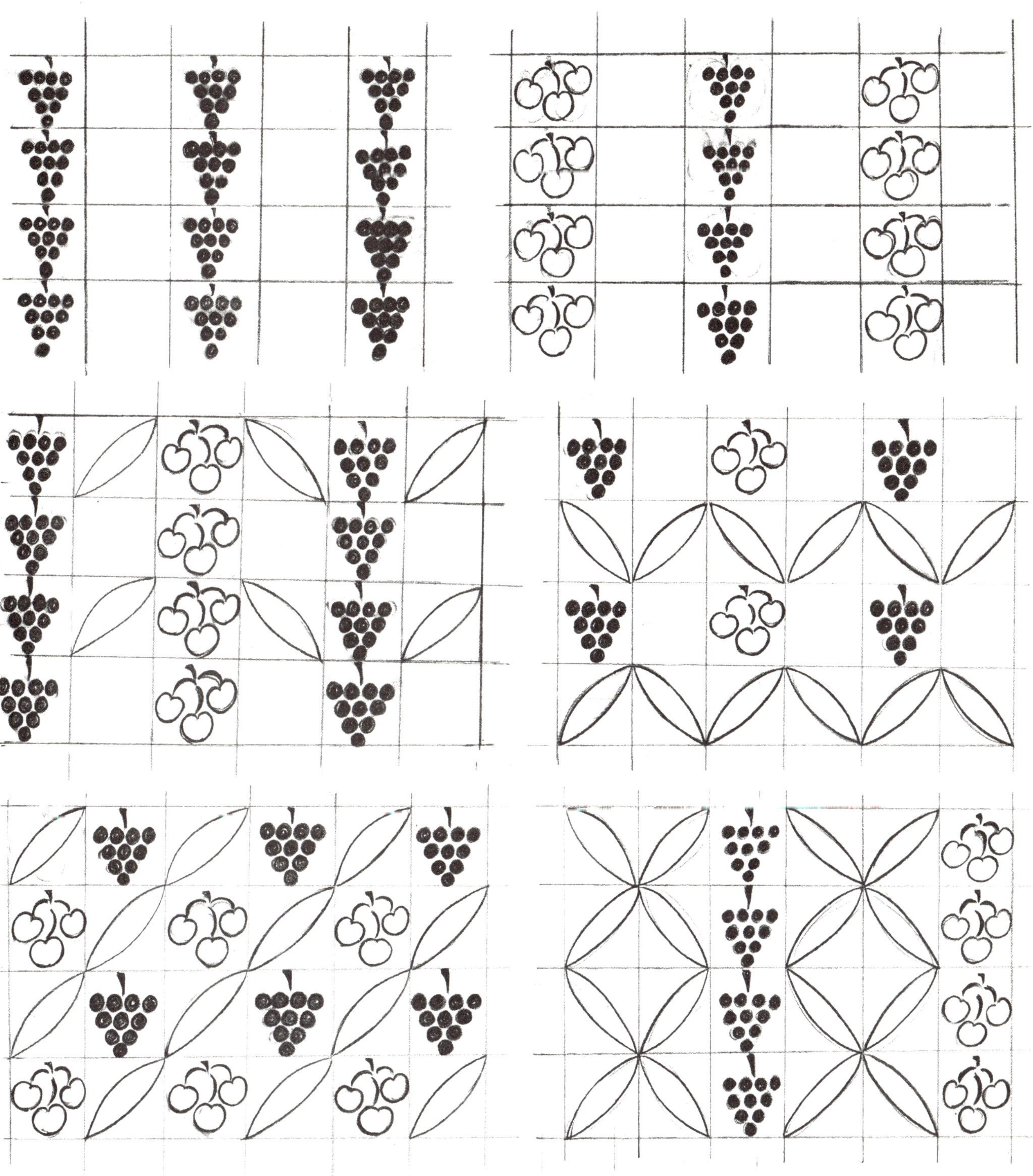

When you have gained confidence in laying out a pattern, you could print your designs with potato blocks, lino blocks or stencils.

Start with a simple motif and work towards something more adventurous, varying the design with the use of colour.

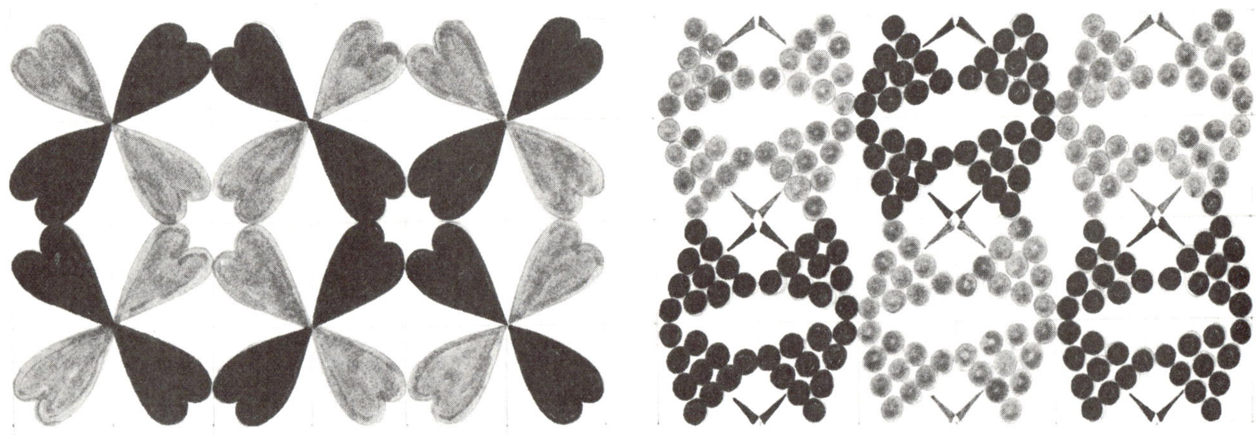

For a more complex pattern on a larger scale, it is a good idea to make a diagram on graph paper to work out where the repeats will occur, using symbols for the different motifs. The example below is a small section of the pattern worked out in the diagram on the left.

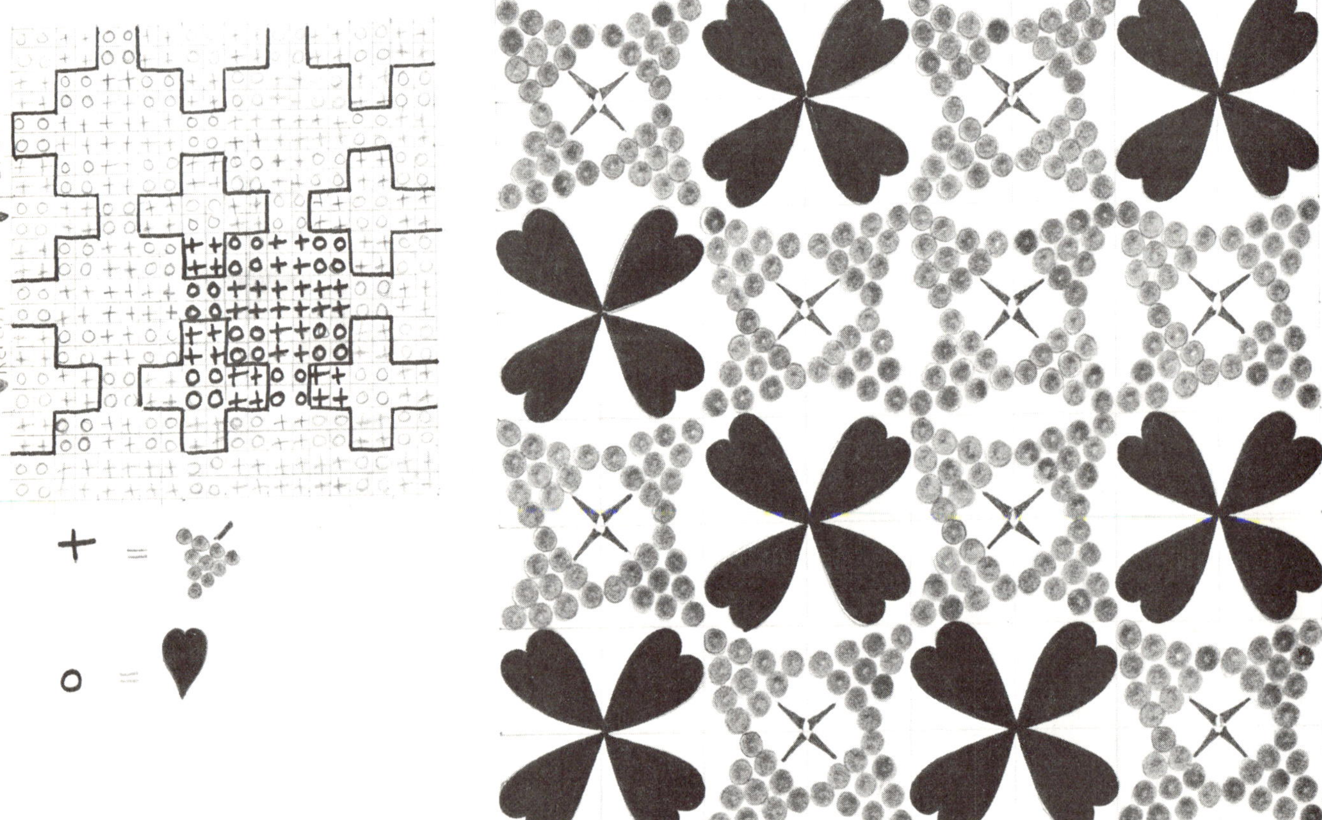

Interlocking patterns

Now try experimenting with interlocking patterns. This needs a considerable amount of accuracy. I suggest making a stencil of your motif. Later, the pattern could be transferred onto fabric by the silk screen process.

A simple example of an interlocking motif, showing the effect of different tone or colour combinations. This one could be applied with a potato print or stencil.

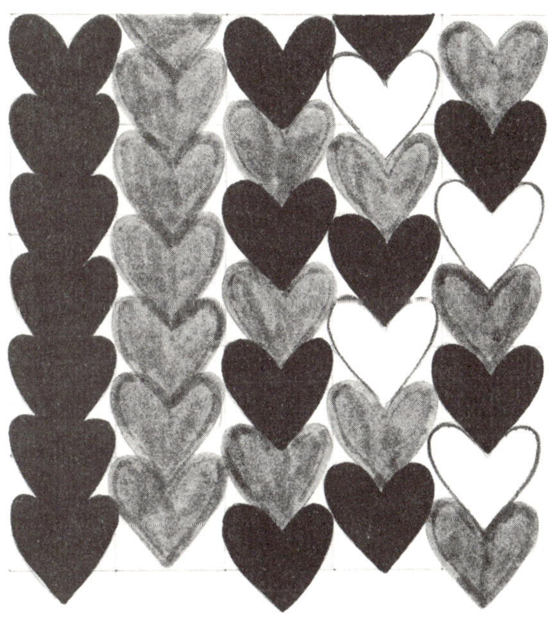

The patterns below not only interlock, but the negative, white space is of equal value to the positive, black motif.

Interlocking patterns can be printed in blocks but it is necessary to work out first where the repeats will occur.

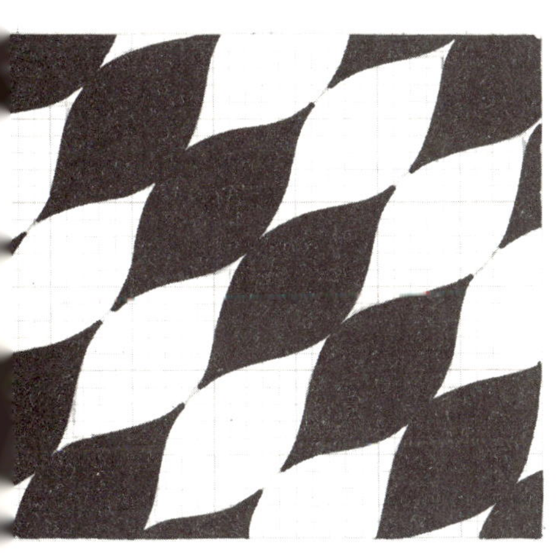

Geometric patterns based on circles

An enormous variety of patterns can be evolved from circles.

Draw the first circle. Then, keeping the same radius, place the point of the compasses anywhere on the circumference and draw an arc across the circle. Move the point to where the arc meets the circumference and draw a second arc. Continue to move round the circle in this way until you have completed a six-petal 'flower' motif.

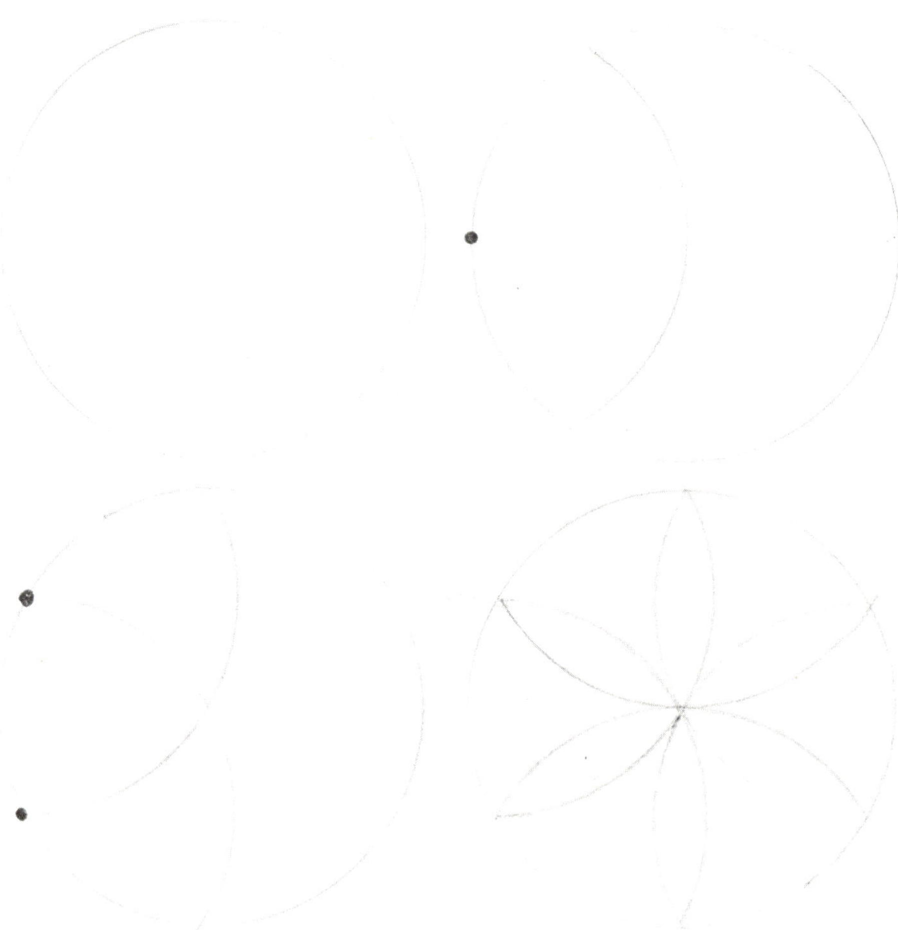

Now place the point of the compasses on the circumference exactly half way between two of the petals and work around the circle again, as before, till you have twelve petals, overlapping in the centre.

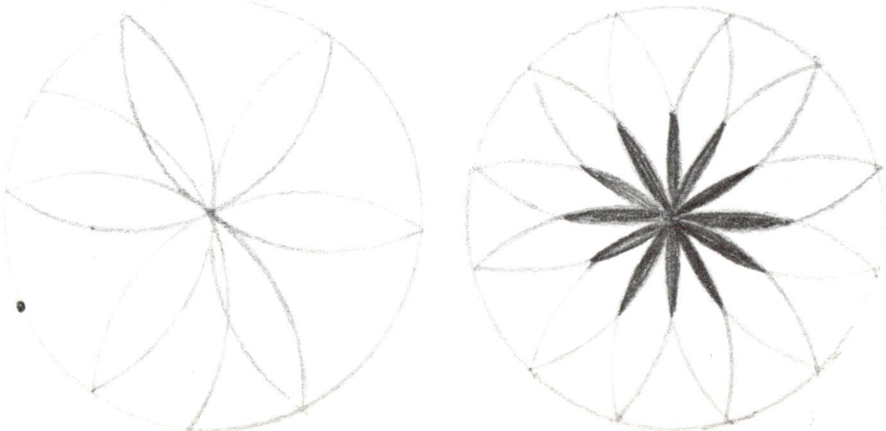

You can continue to build up the design like this with any number of petals; but for a large number it is easier to start with a larger circle.

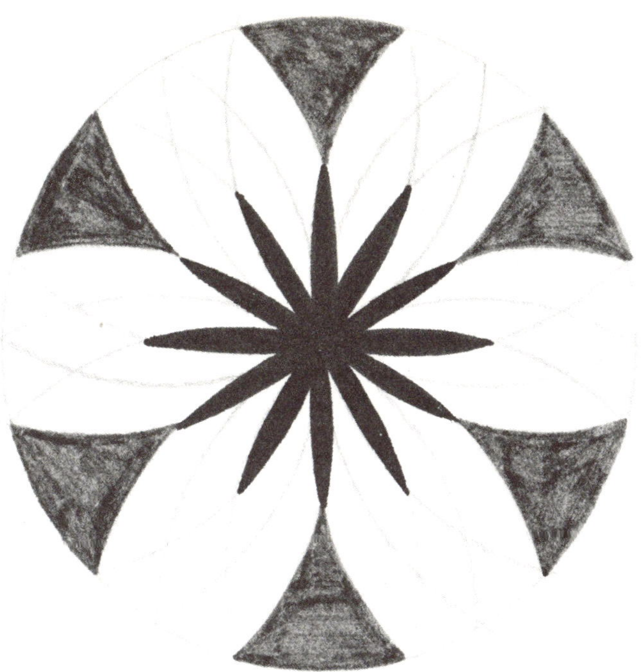

Instead of finishing each arc where it meets the edge of the circle you can continue it to form another circle. More complex patterns can be built up in this way, on the same principle as the petal design.

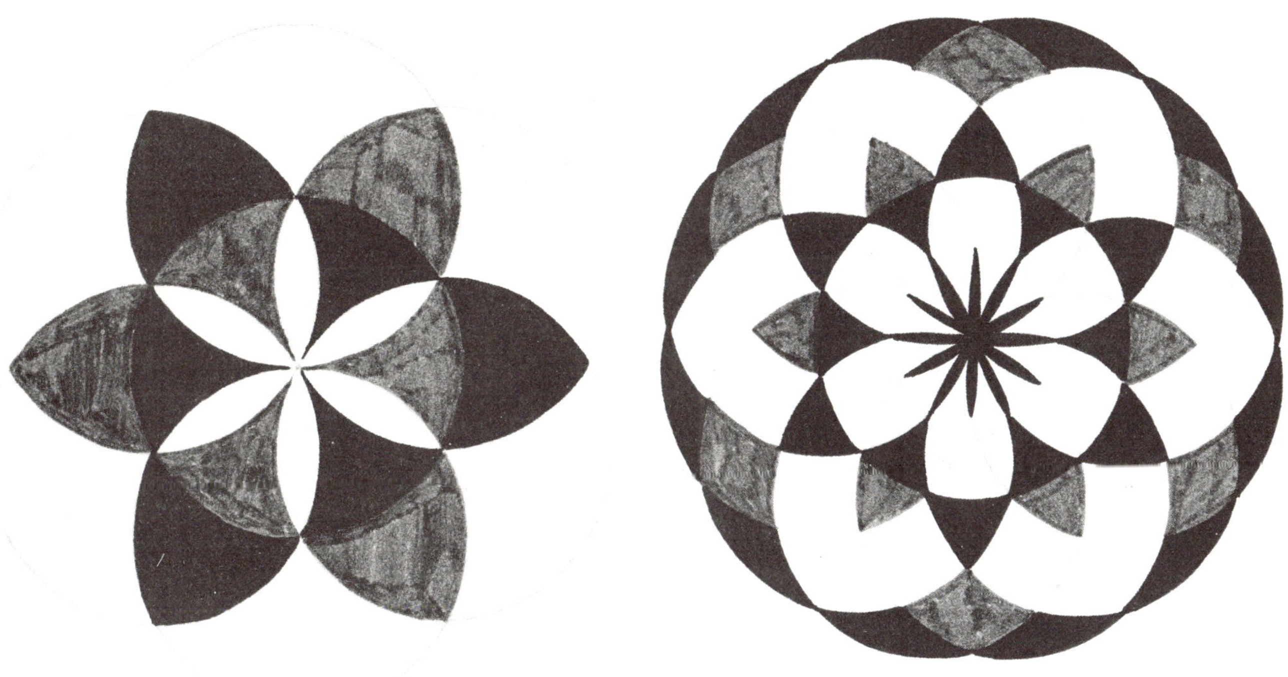

You can make your designs as complex as you like. By filling in different areas, different patterns will emerge.

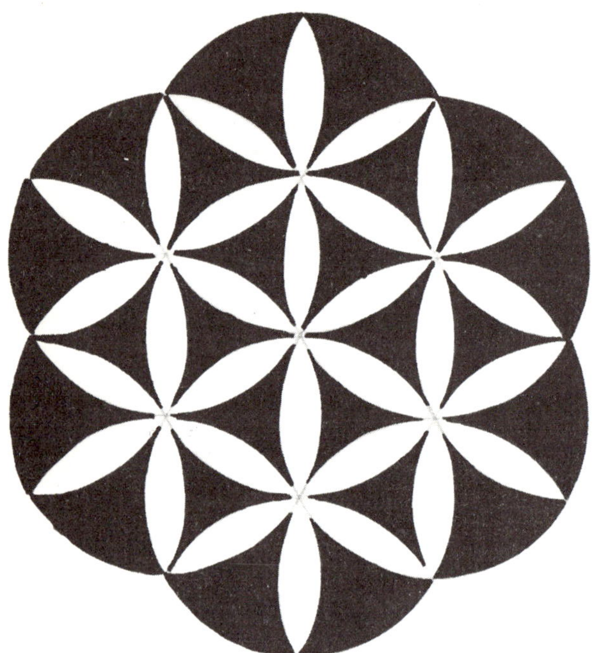

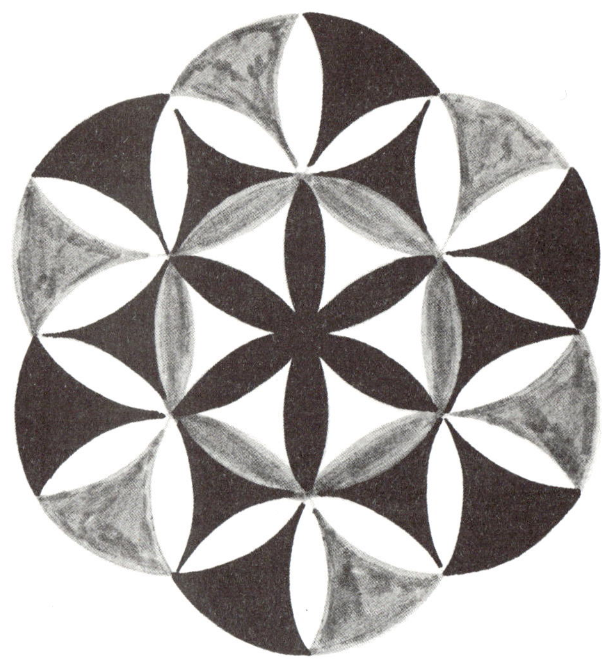

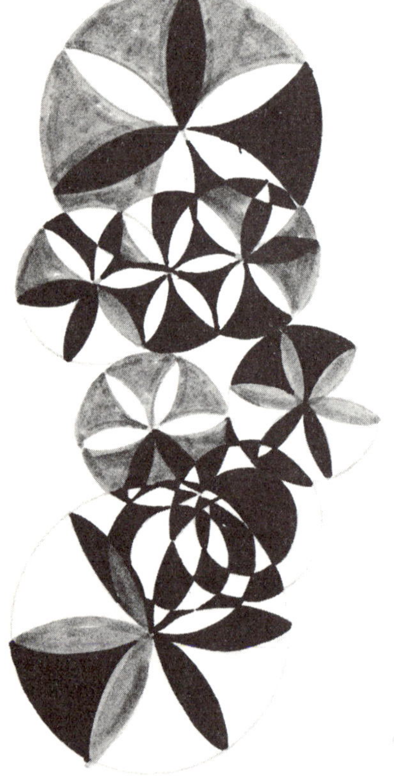

A more abstract, less formal pattern can be evolved by mixing circles of different sizes.

This pattern is made of three overlapping circles, each with twelve petals as shown on the previous page.

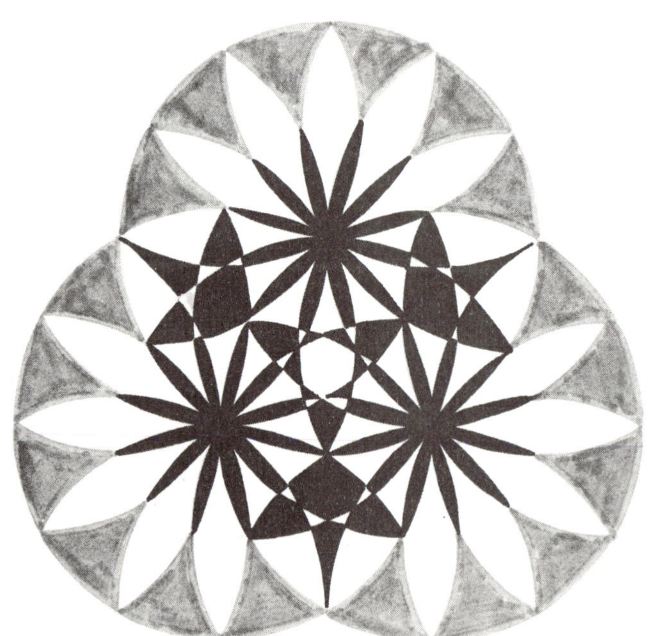

Try combining circles with straight lines. Mark off equal segments on the circumference of a circle with the compasses, as before; then join these points with lines in different ways.

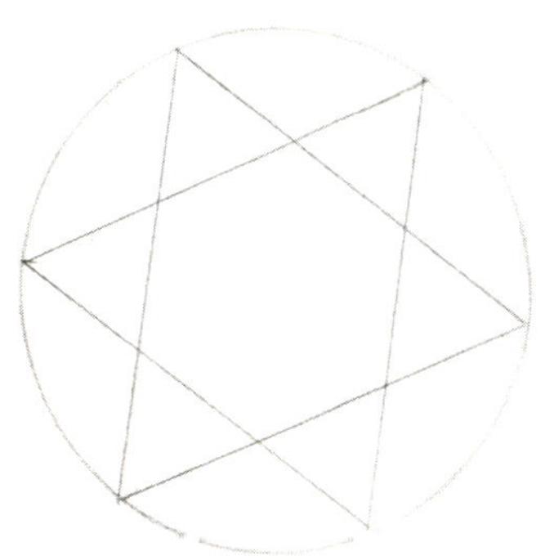
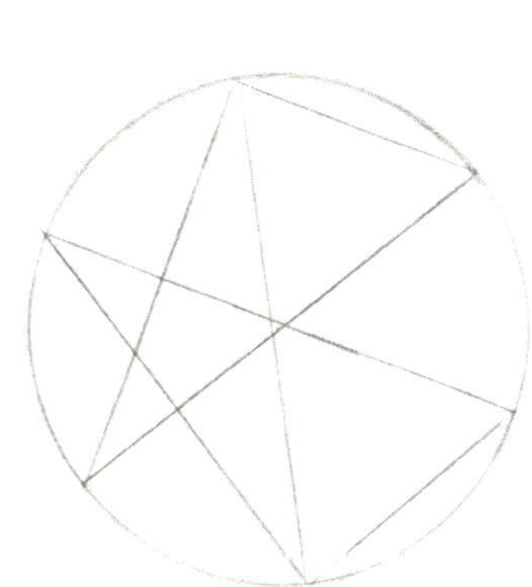
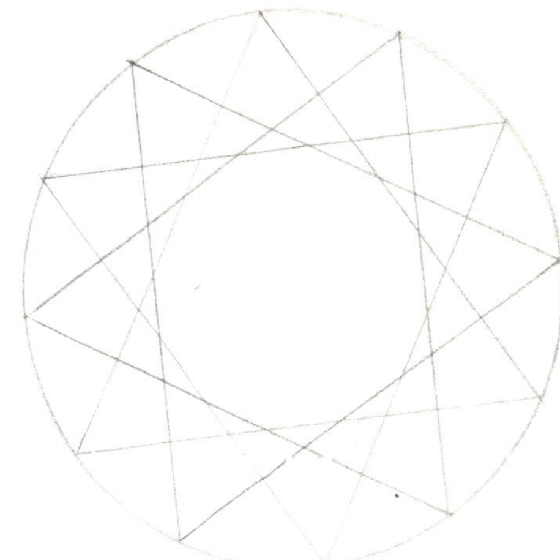

All these patterns are basically simple, but with the addition of blocking in or colour you can achieve a fantastic variety.

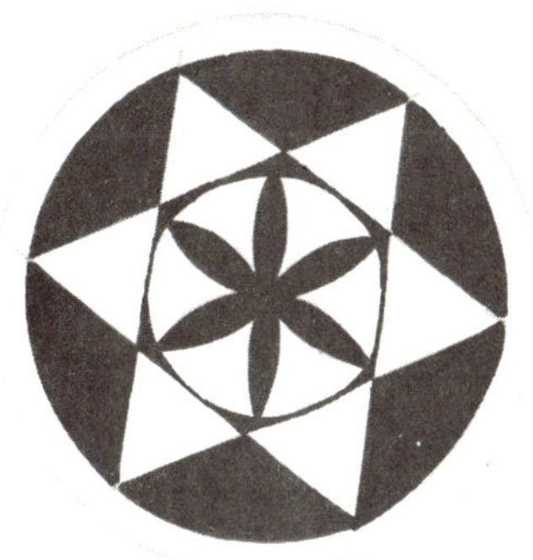
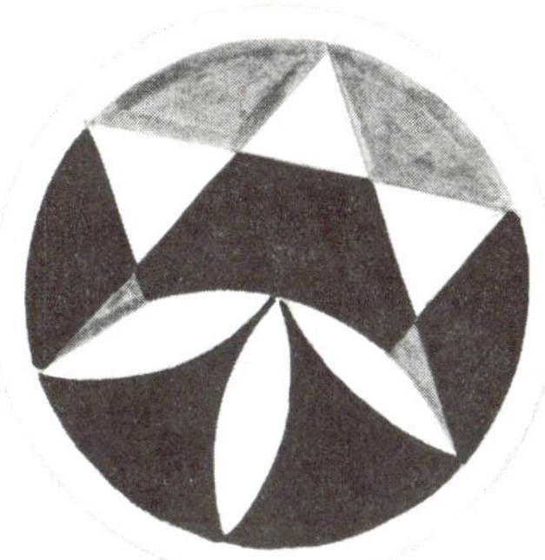
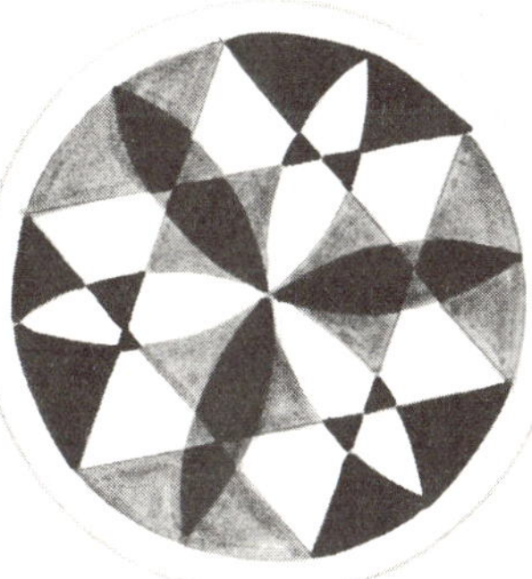

This is a mixture of 'flower' and 'star' patterns.

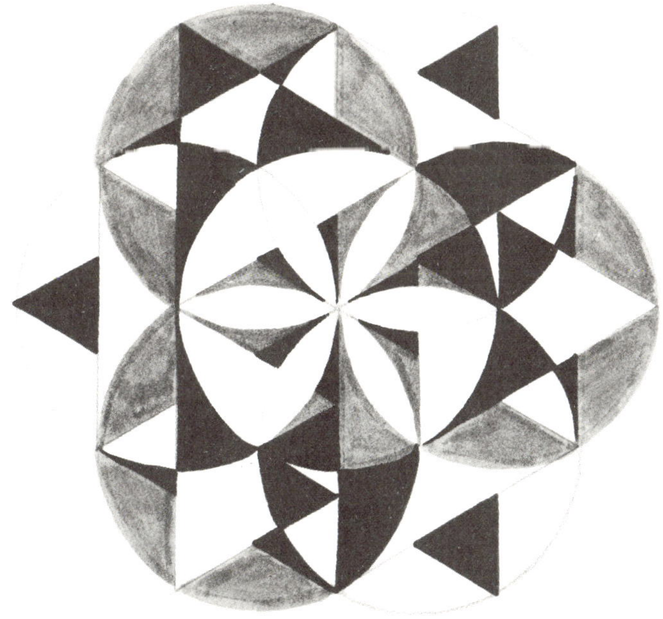

Filling a given area

One way to fill an area with pattern is to work outwards from the centre. These designs are complete in themselves. They are not suitable for all-over repeating patterns, but could be used as motifs to be incorporated in a larger design.

The first two show the most obvious way to fill a space, starting from the centre. Experiment with more complex patterns in circles, either drawn freehand or using ruler and compasses.

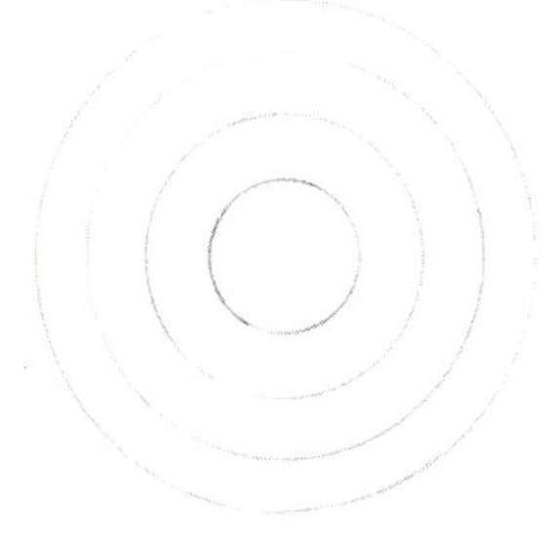
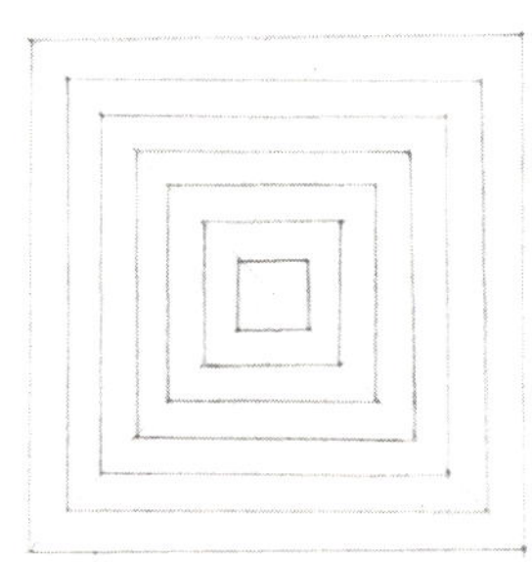

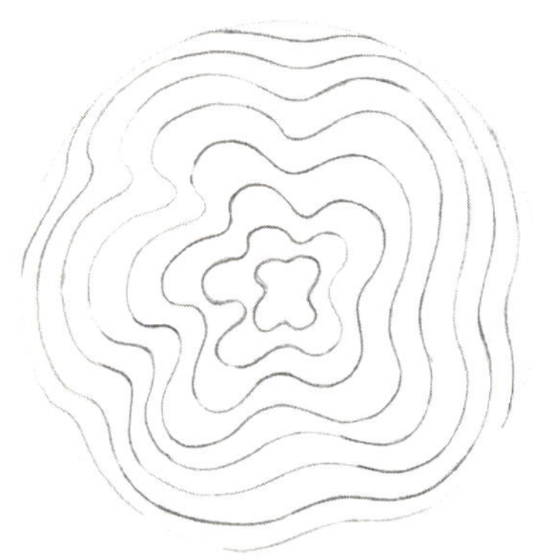
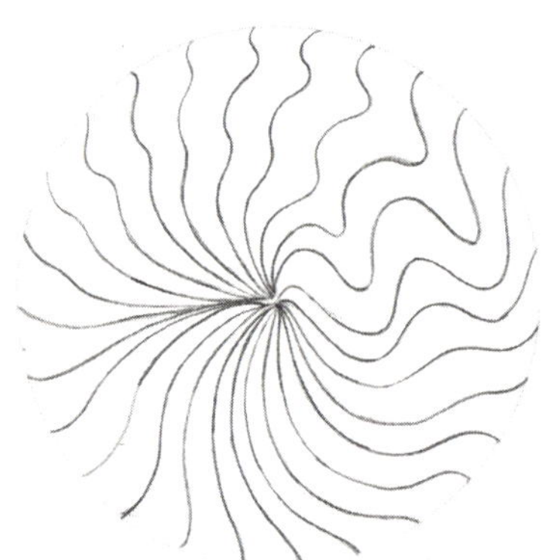
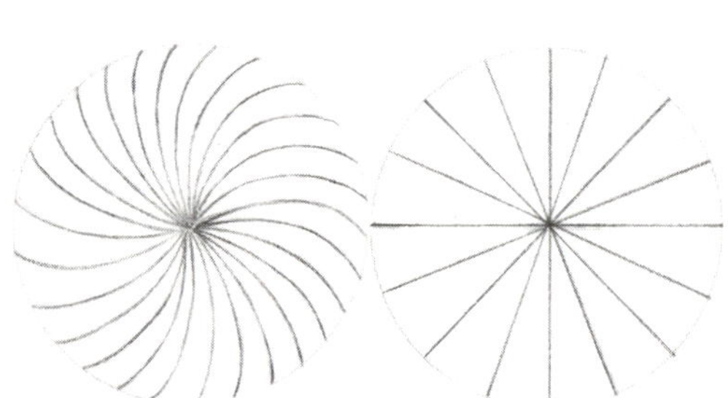

These patterns were drawn free-hand, having first measured and marked the centre and other necessary guide-lines. If you want to transfer your patterns to cushions, rugs, plates, etc. they can be worked out more accurately. To increase the area with another band of pattern, draw a larger circle round the first one from the same centre point.

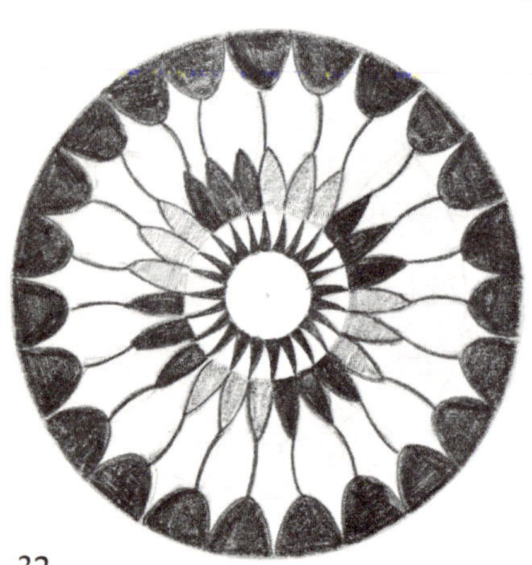
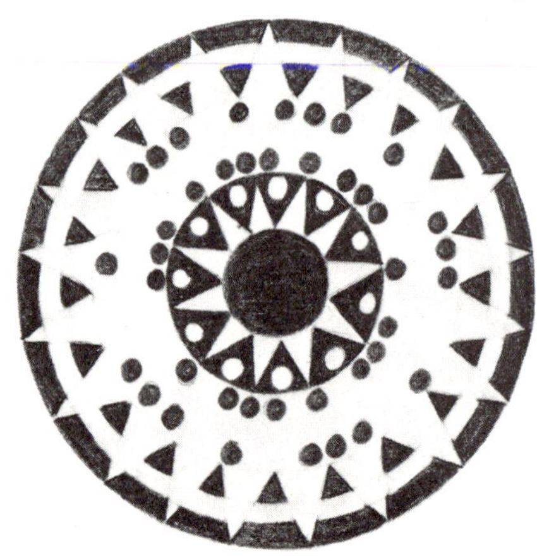
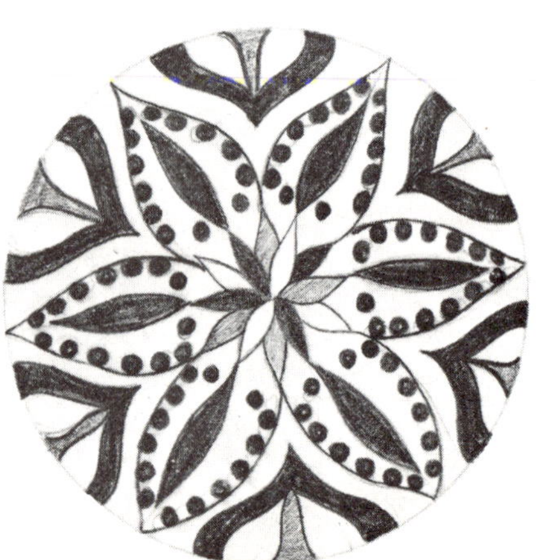

Some examples of working out from the centre of a square, showing both formal and abstract patterns.

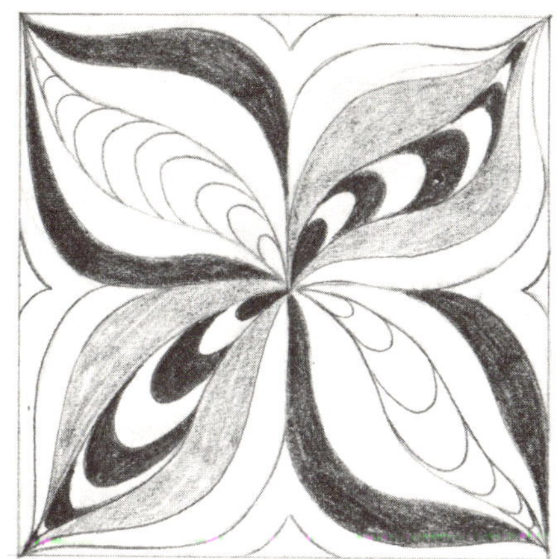

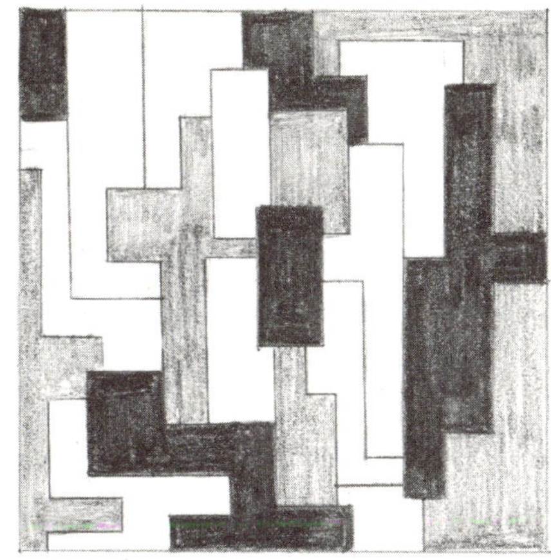

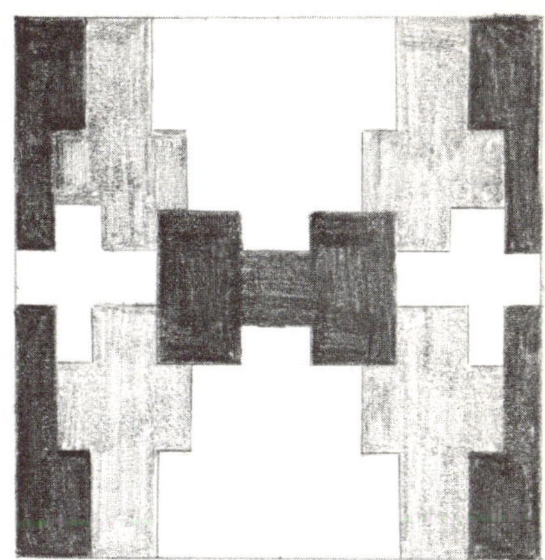

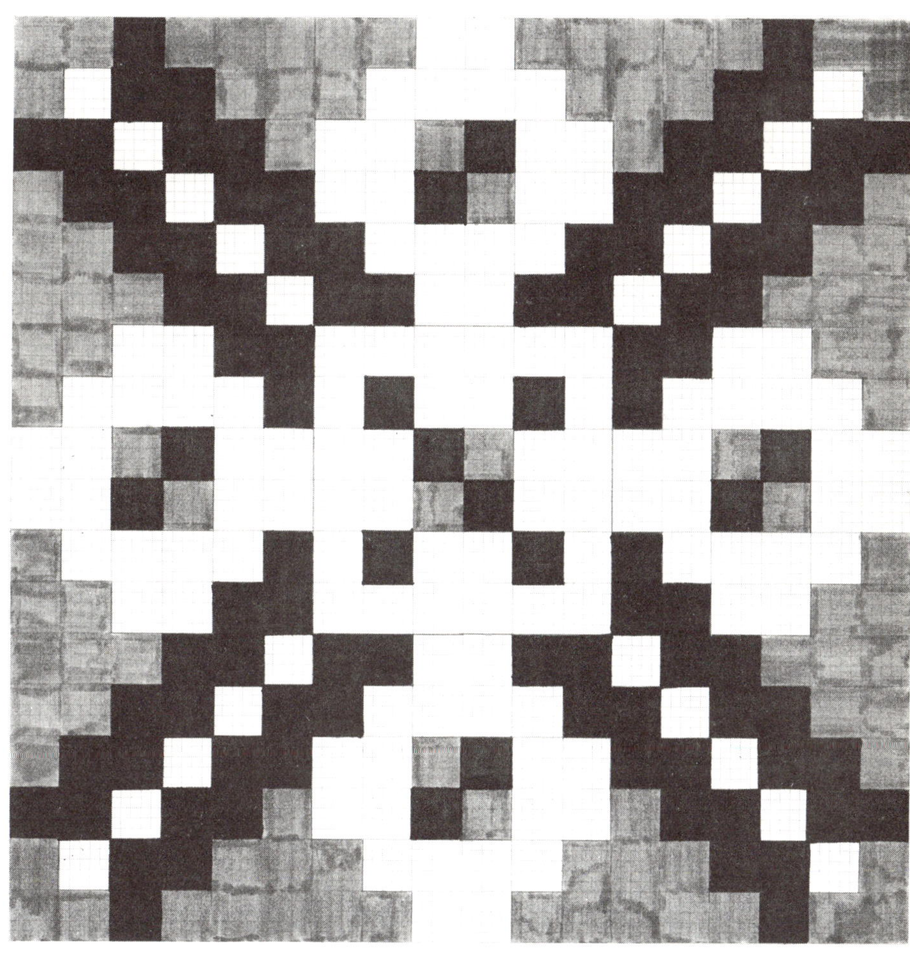

Here are some more non-repeating patterns within a defined area, working now from side to side or from corner to corner.

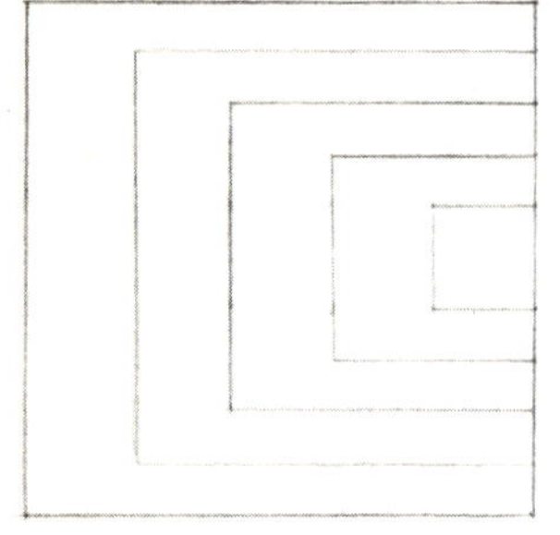
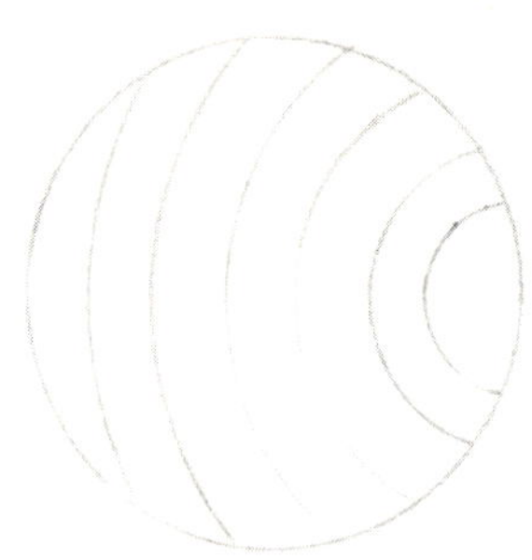
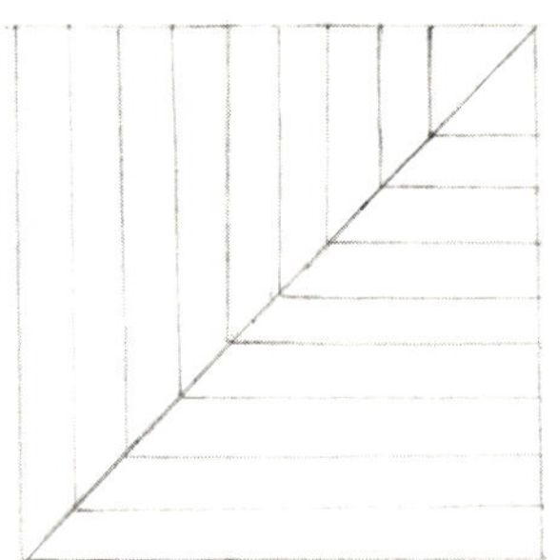
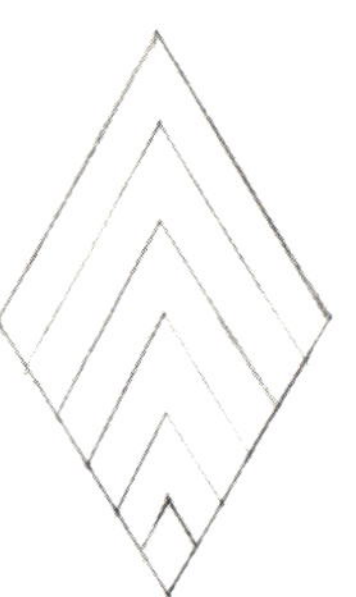

An abstract pattern in a hexagon, built up from a small shape on the right.

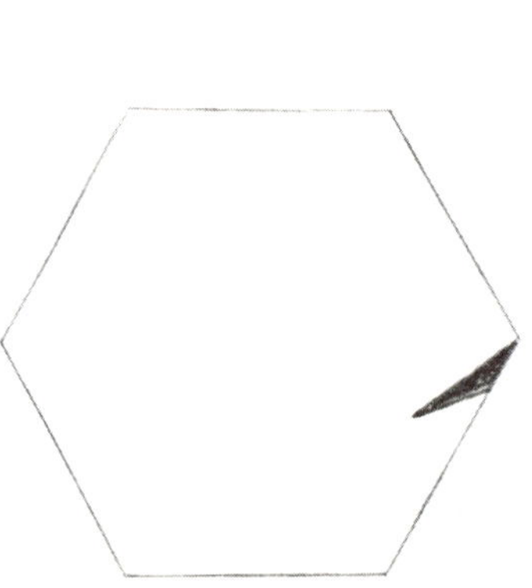
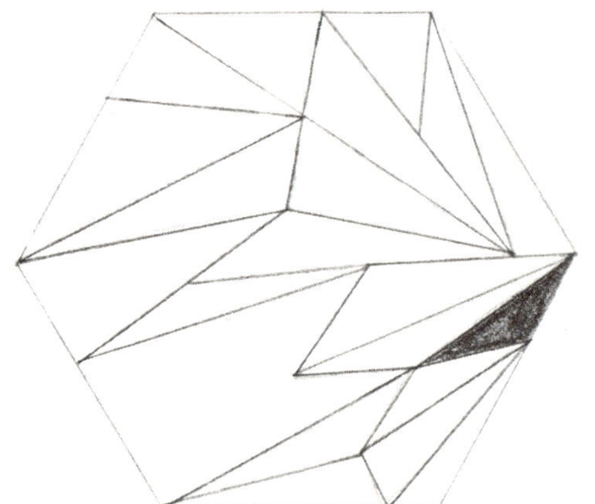

Patterns can be developed in a formal way, or at random or worked from both sides at once towards the centre.

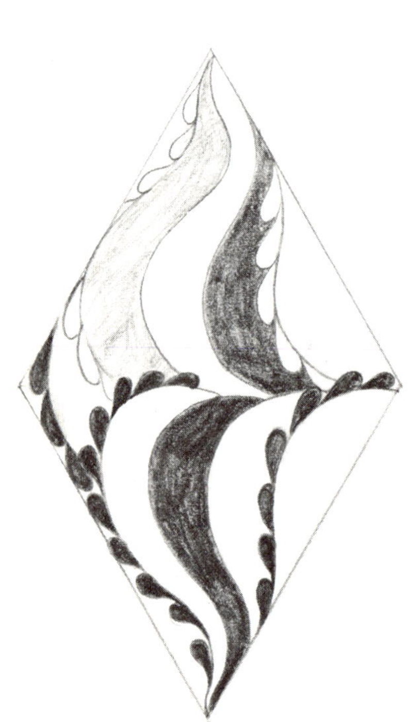
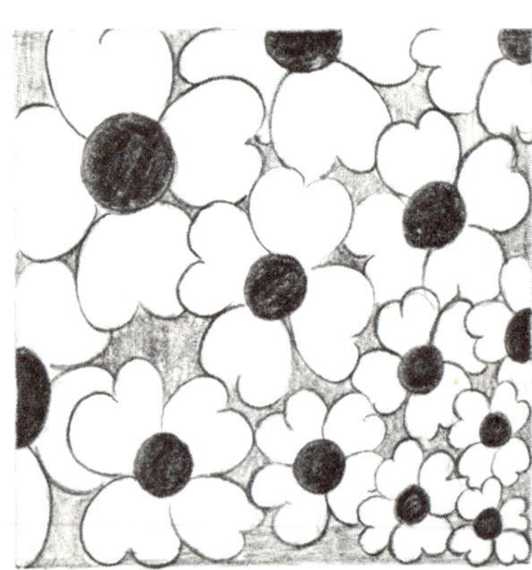
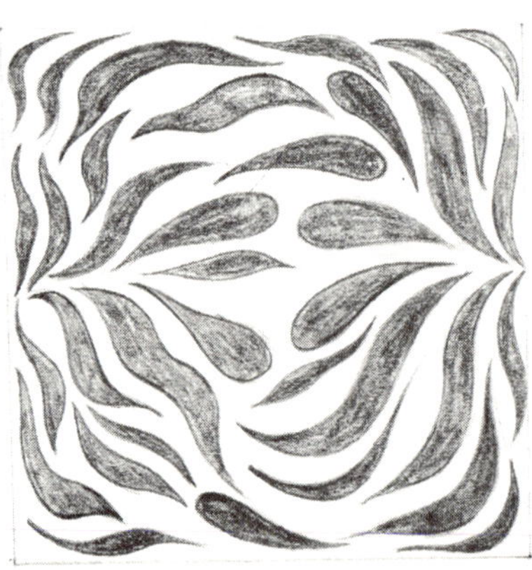

Further ideas for patterns to fill a variety of given shapes. You will probably find that the shape dictates the sort of pattern you decide to draw.

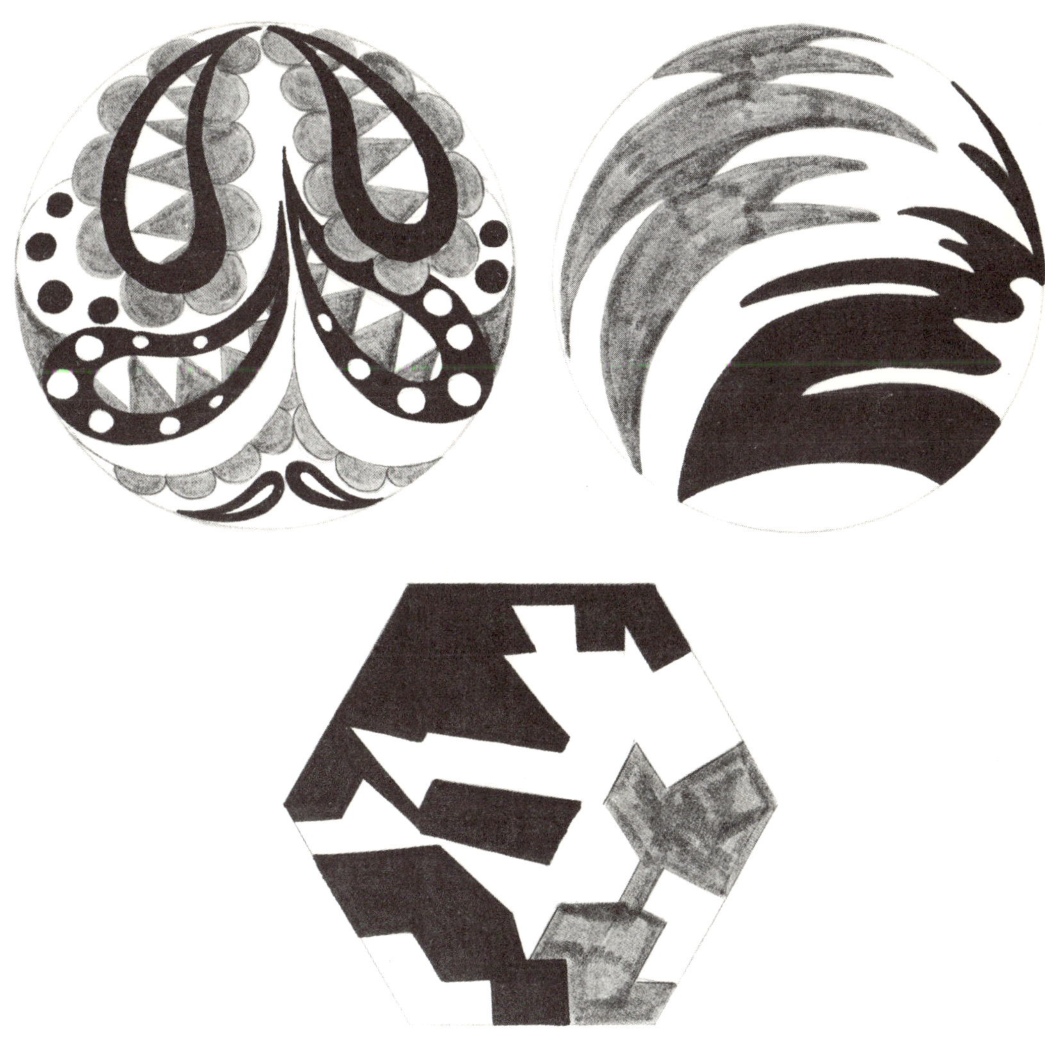

This way of filling areas with pattern can be used to decorate pots and other three-dimensional objects or for embroidery (see also pages 44–7).

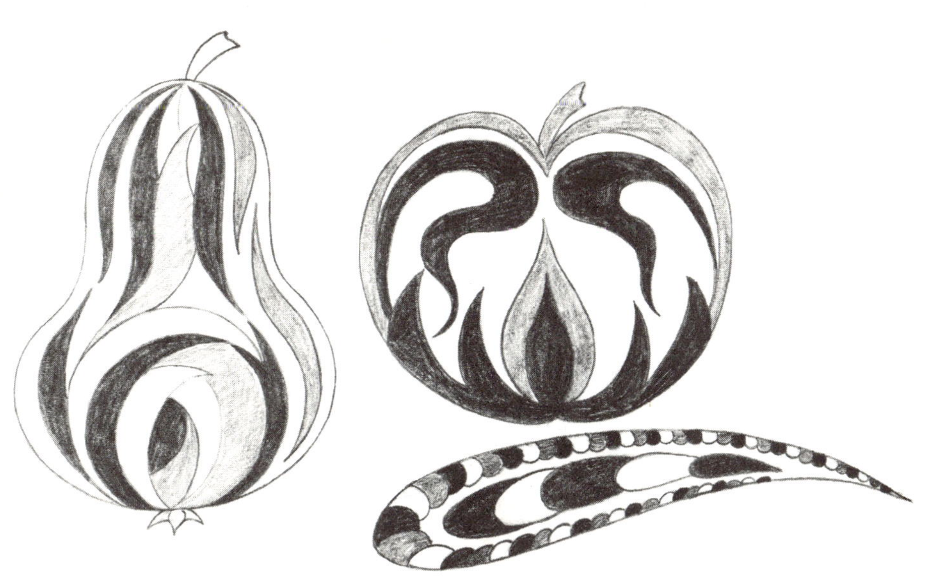

Ideas from the environment

You can find pattern everywhere you look: in buildings (brickwork, windows, ironwork); in nature (flowers, insects, shells, branches); around the house (domestic implements, tiles, the weave of a carpet, a stain on the wall). Look at road intersections, telegraph wires, fields, the night sky, clouds, reflections and ripples in water, waves breaking on the shore.

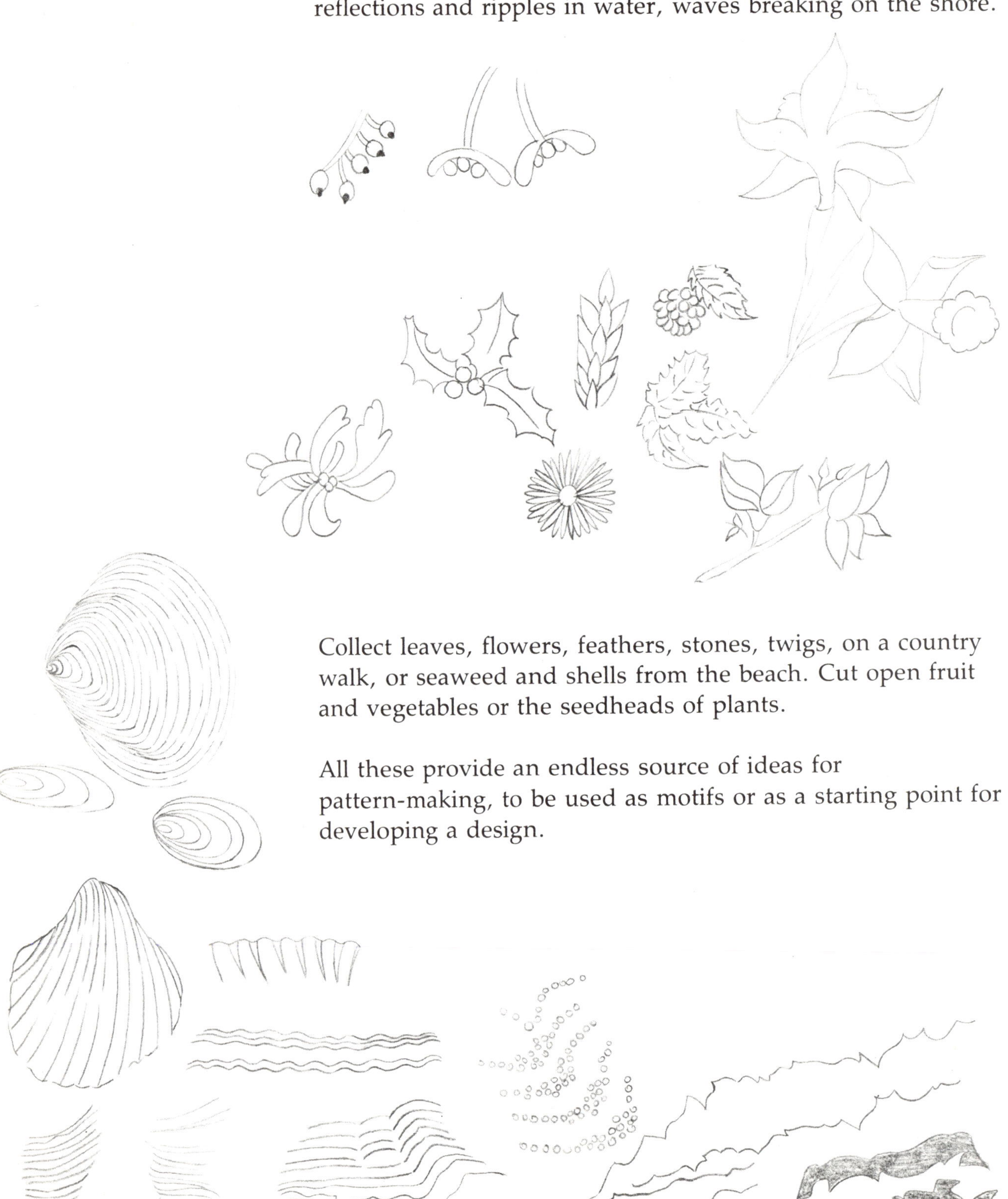

Collect leaves, flowers, feathers, stones, twigs, on a country walk, or seaweed and shells from the beach. Cut open fruit and vegetables or the seedheads of plants.

All these provide an endless source of ideas for pattern-making, to be used as motifs or as a starting point for developing a design.

Here are a few examples of ideas from nature that I have started to develop into patterns.

The shapes below were taken from marks on stones. They can be used individually as decoration or as the basis for a repeating pattern, using tracing paper to repeat the shape accurately.

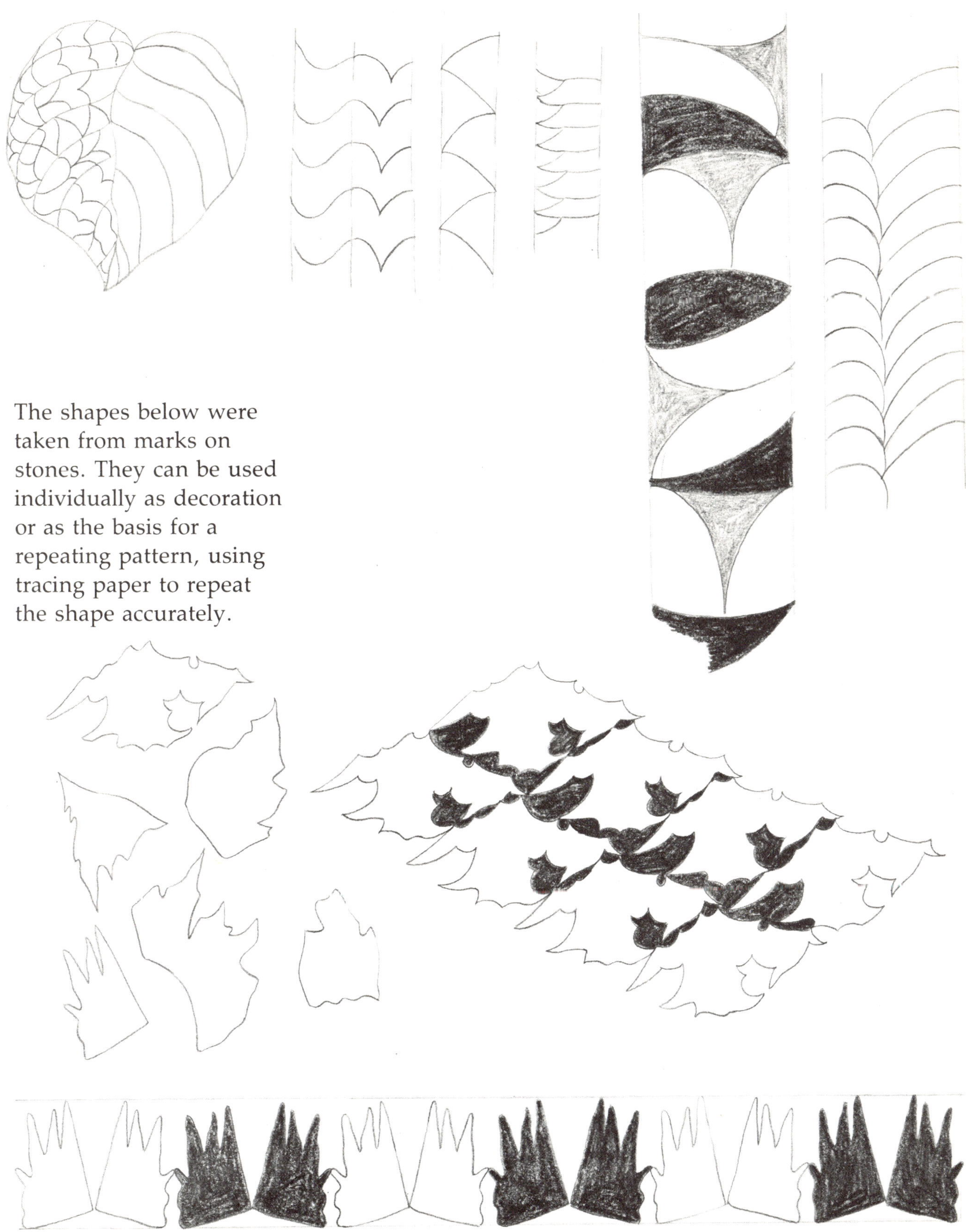

Start by drawing from life if possible; then develop a stylised design from your drawing.

Alternatively, you can trace a subject from a book and develop your pattern from it.

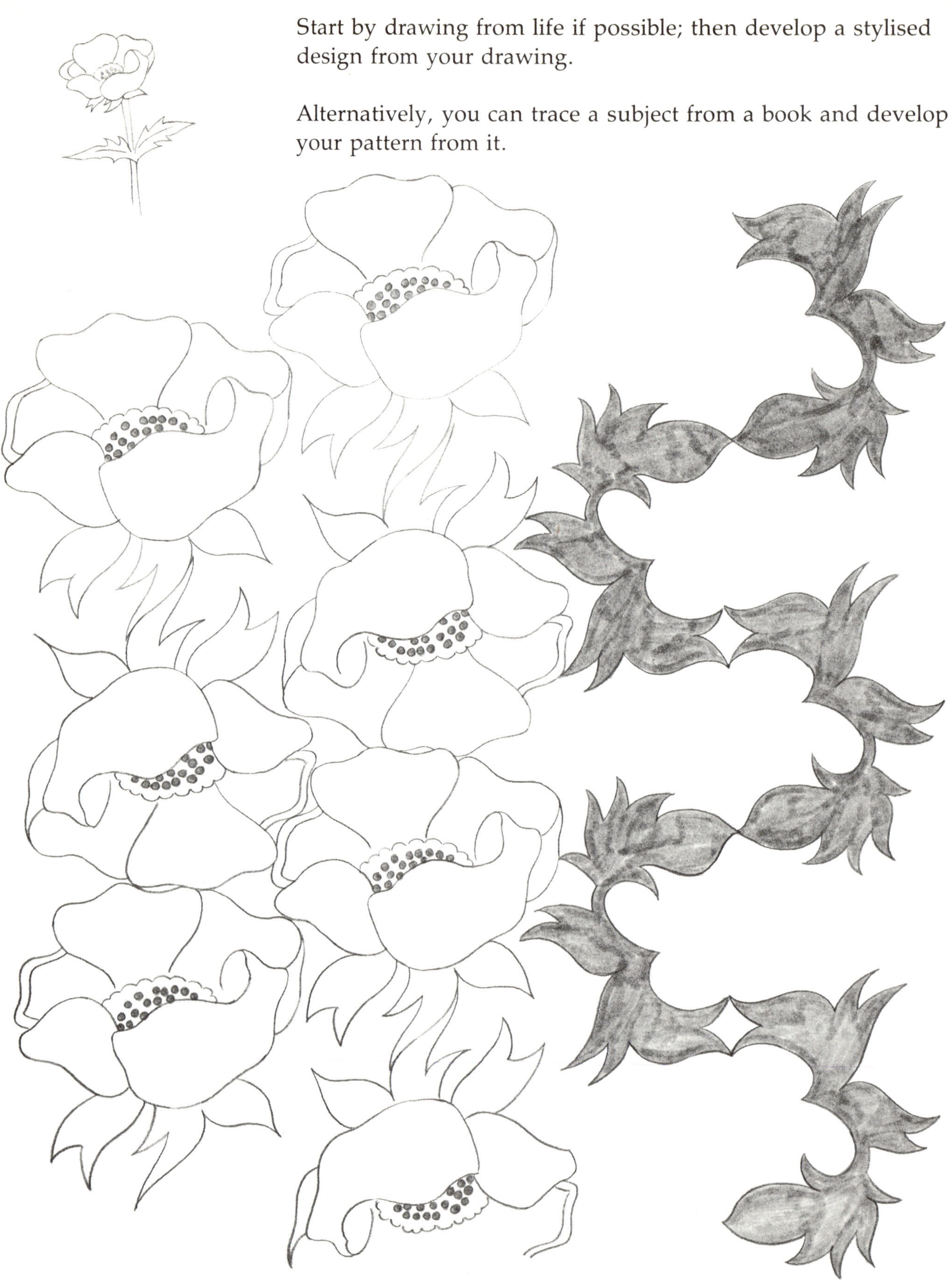

This stylised repeating pattern was developed from the buttercup flower and its leaves opposite.

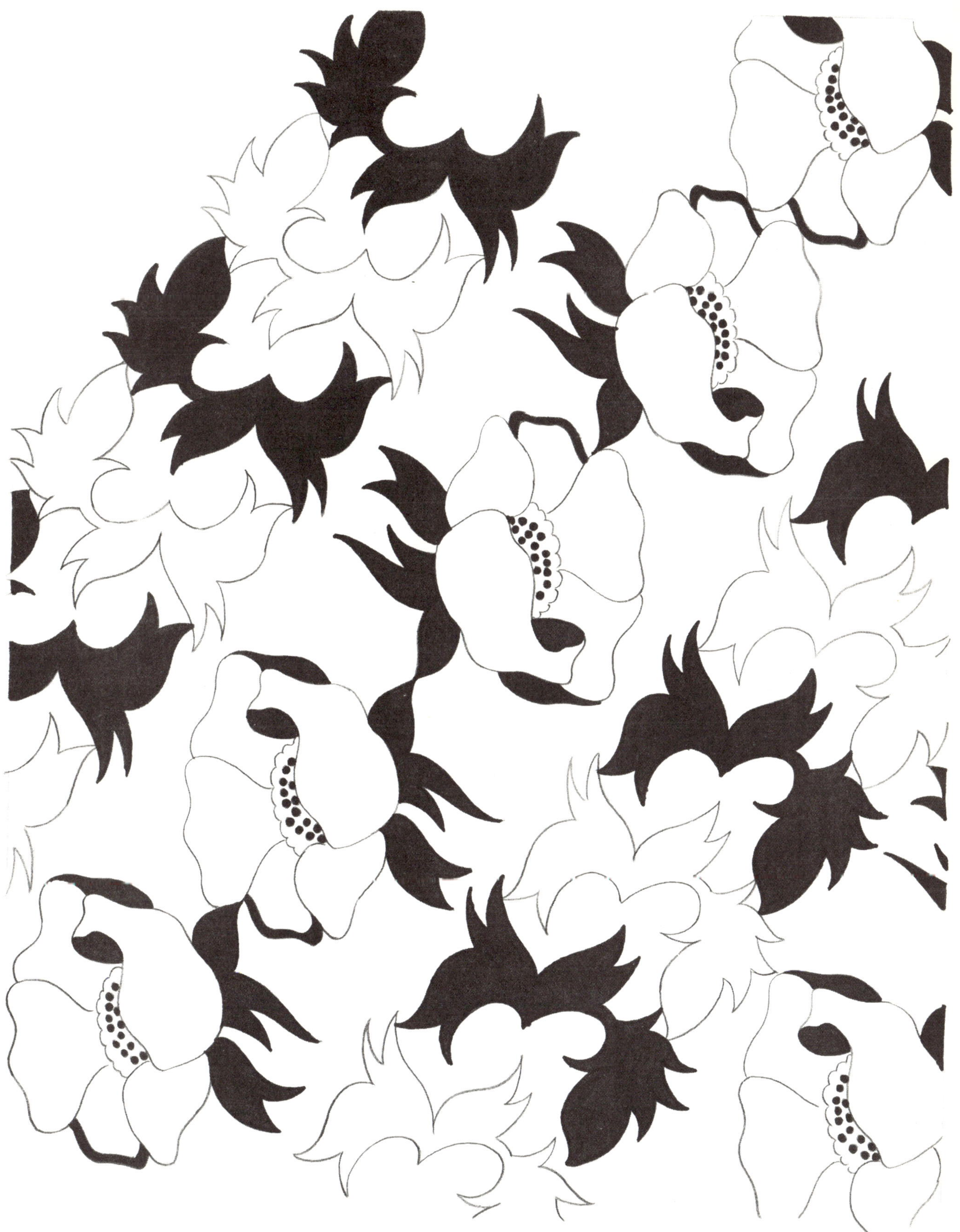

This set of patterns was inspired by a cauliflower cut in half. First I made some preliminary sketches, and from these I made up my motifs and combined them in a variety of different ways.

Ideas from the environment can also be used in any of the design forms described earlier in the book.

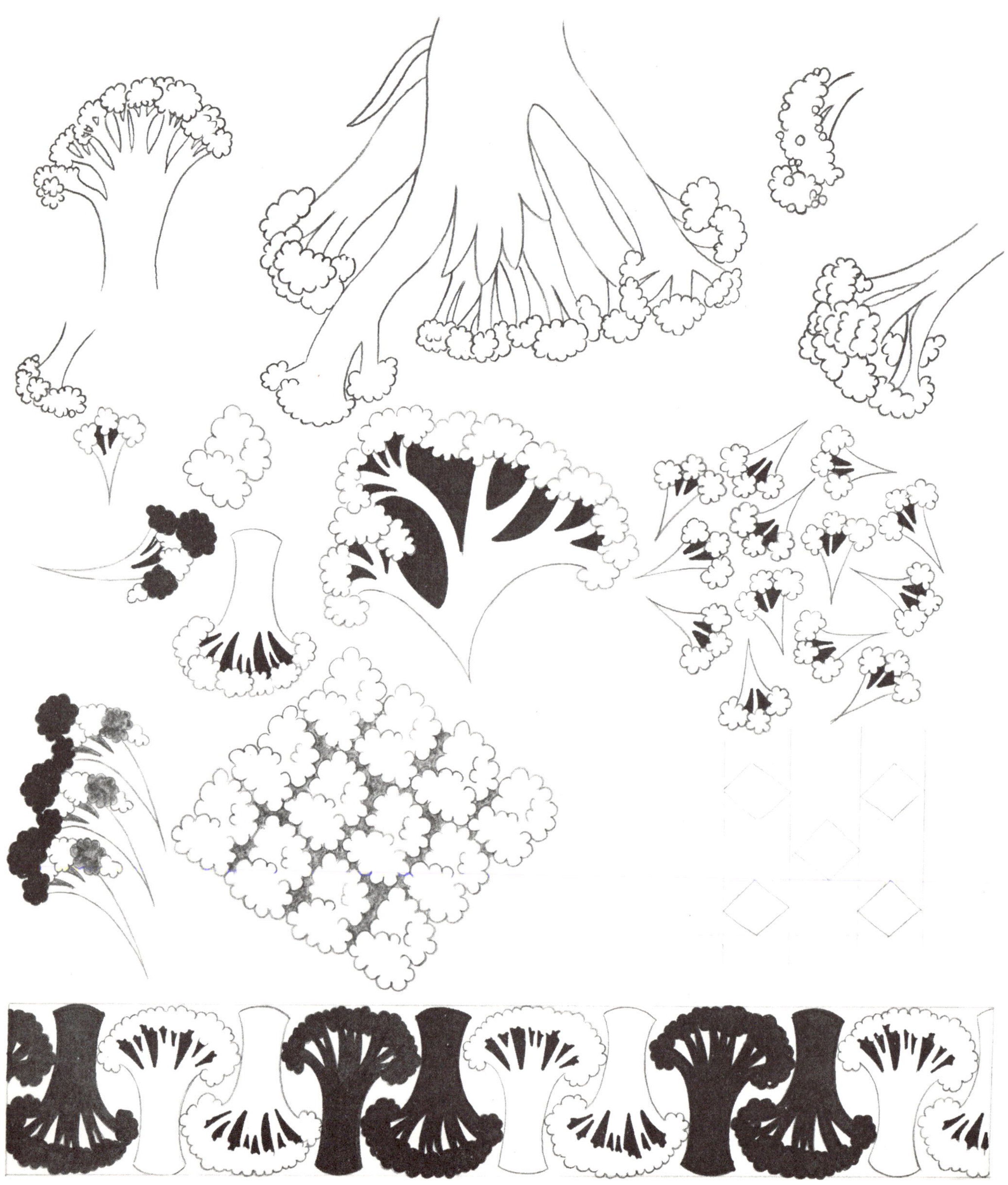

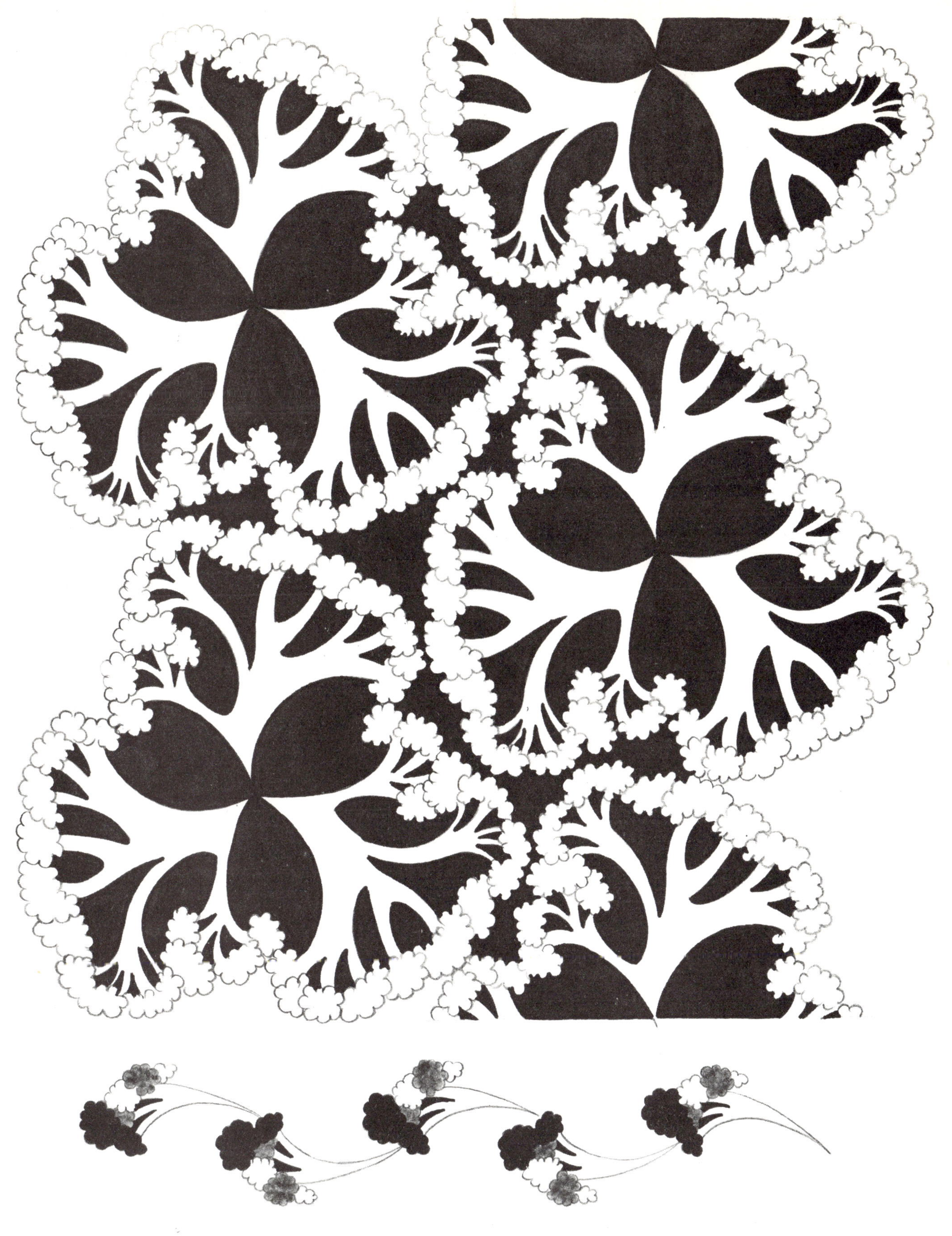

Objects from the kitchen drawer can be the starting point for a pattern. Being hard-edged and regular in shape, they will probably dictate a regular, geometric type of pattern. This one was based on kitchen knives placed end to end.

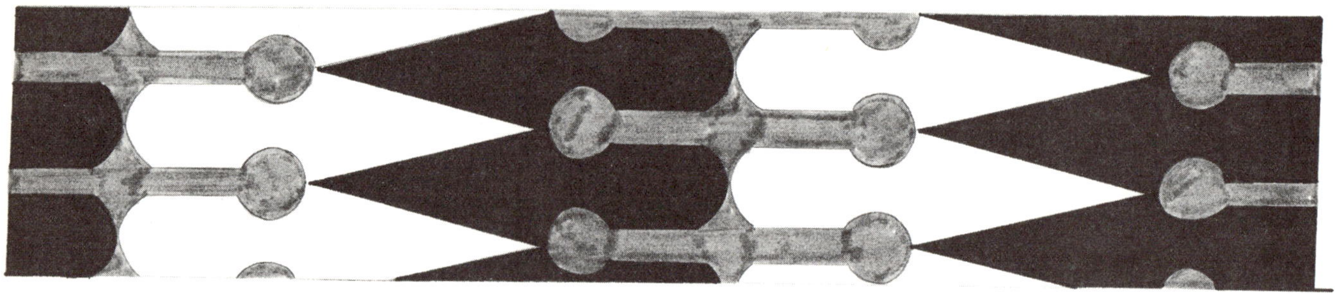

A pattern built up from beaker shapes, using the curve of the rim to dictate the overall shape.

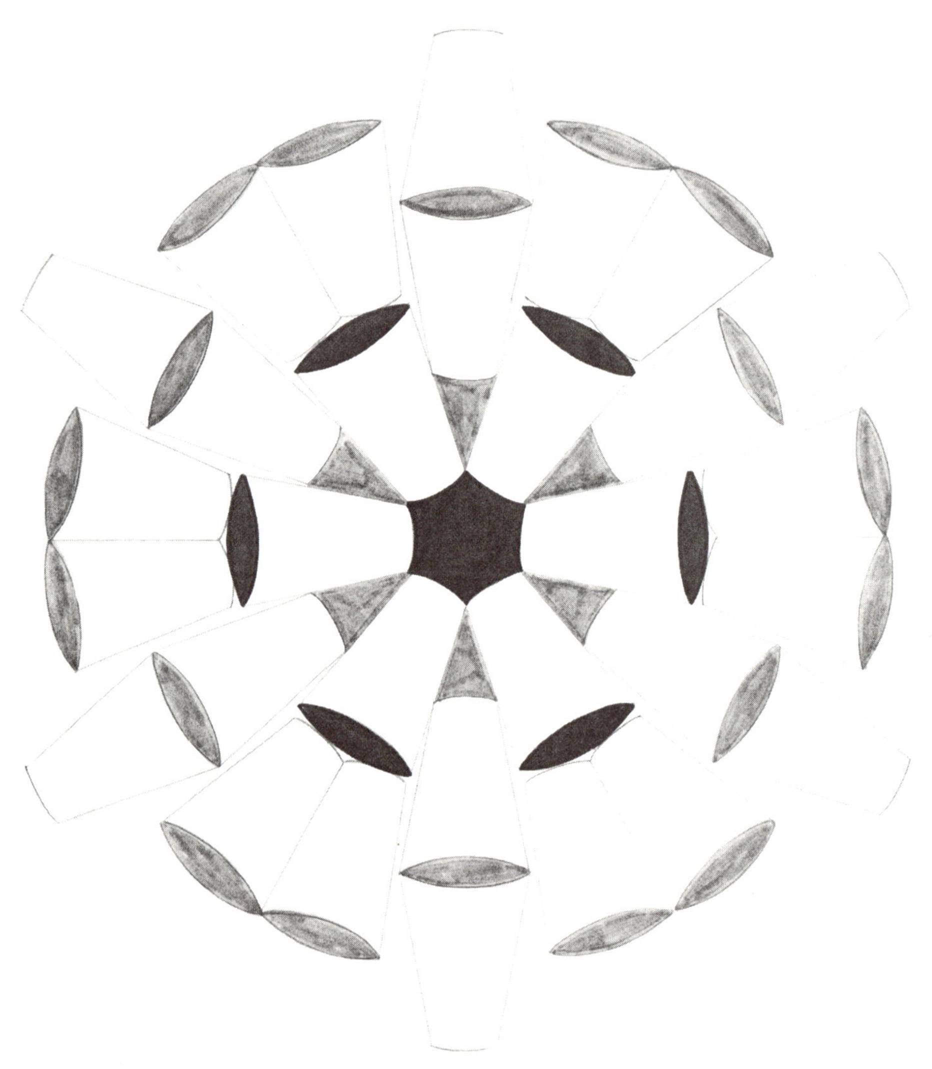

Shapes can be adapted. Here I have used a spoon shape bent to produce a wavy pattern.

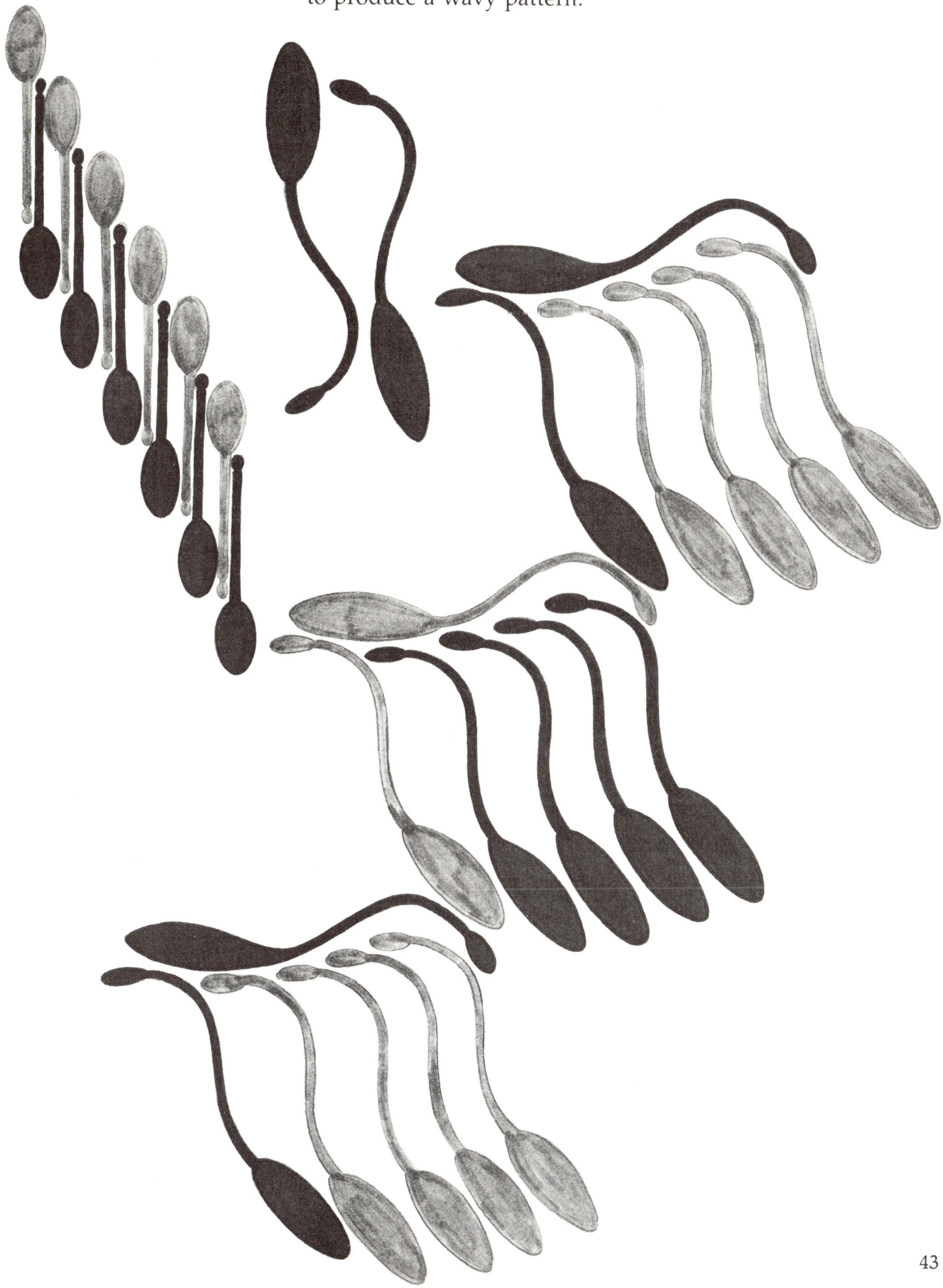

Using your patterns

Having explored the possibilities of pattern-drawing on paper, you can transfer your patterns onto all sorts of surfaces and objects.

First you need to decide what sort of design is best for the surface you want to decorate, and what method you will use to transfer it.

There are no hard and fast rules, but here are a few starting points. As you become more experienced in using pattern, you will be able to judge for yourself which methods to use, and your ability to work free-hand on curving surfaces will improve.

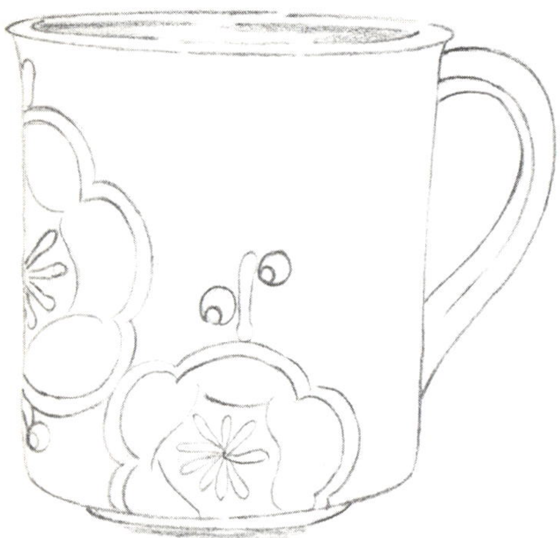

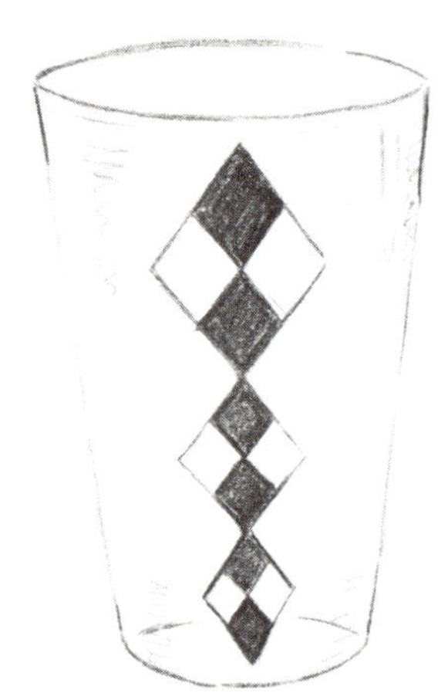

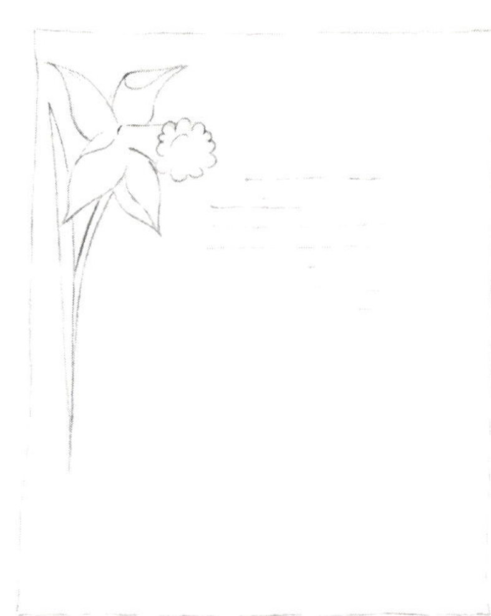

Most continuous patterns are suitable for fabrics, wall papers, wrapping papers. Floral patterns are often the most popular but geometric prints in bright colours can be very exciting. Potato blocks, lino and woodcuts can be used for printing simple motifs; for more complex patterns silk screen is a good method. You could find out more about these techniques from a book on print-making, or join an evening class.

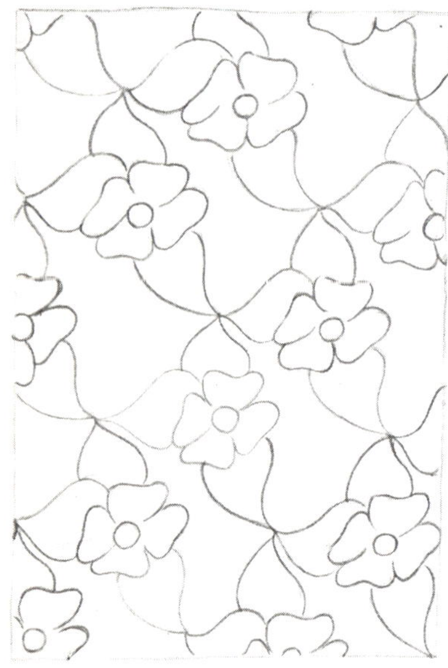

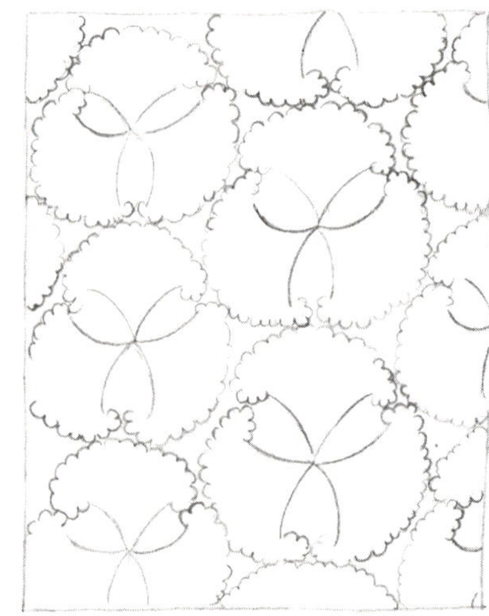

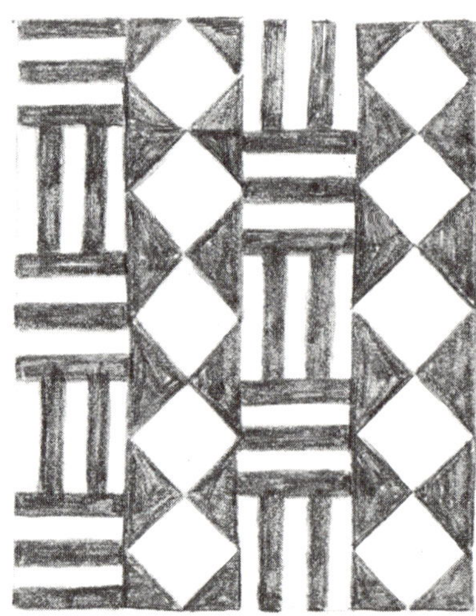

Patterns can also be designed for weaving, rug-making, embroidery and patchwork; for painting directly on to fabric with fabric dyes; for mosaic and marquetry; and for decorating pottery and other three-dimensional objects, as shown on the next two pages.

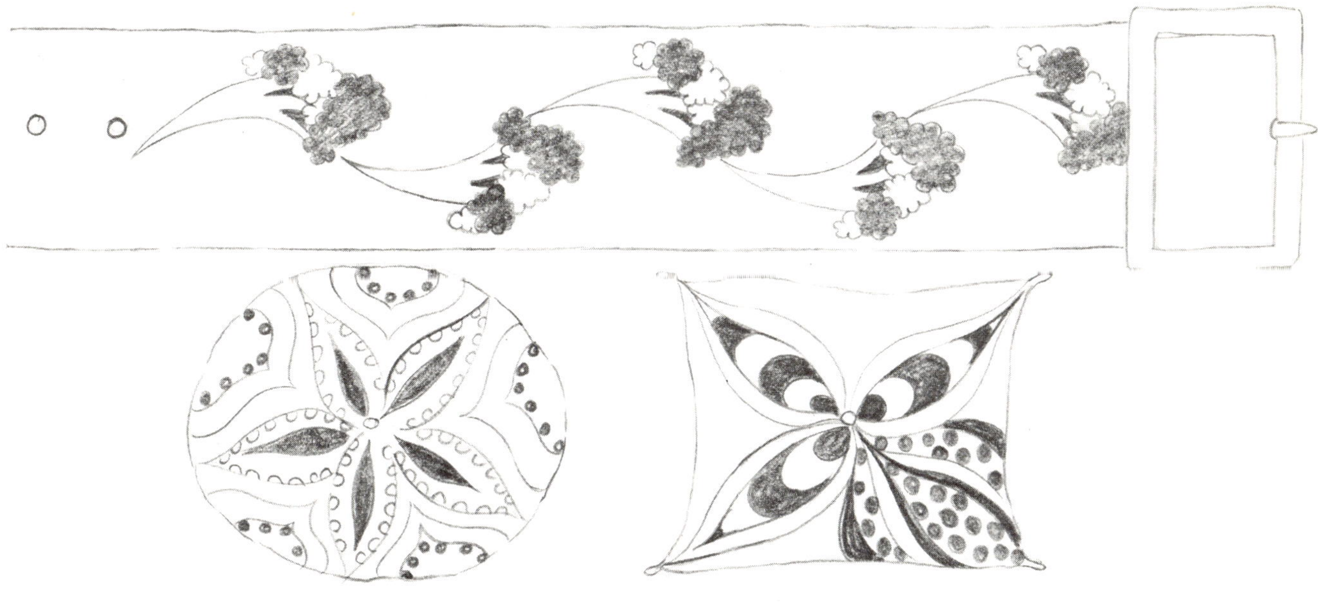

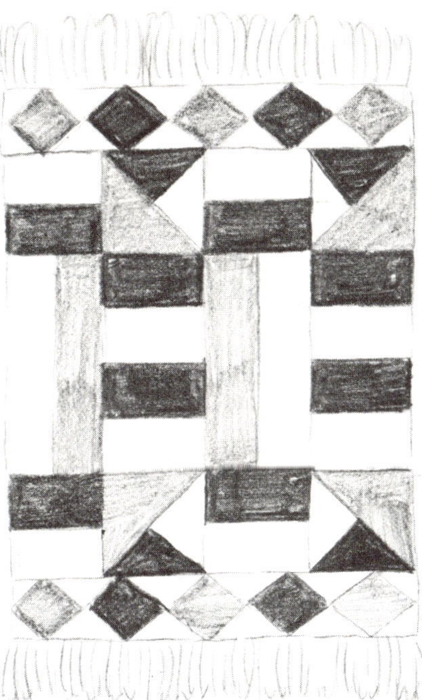

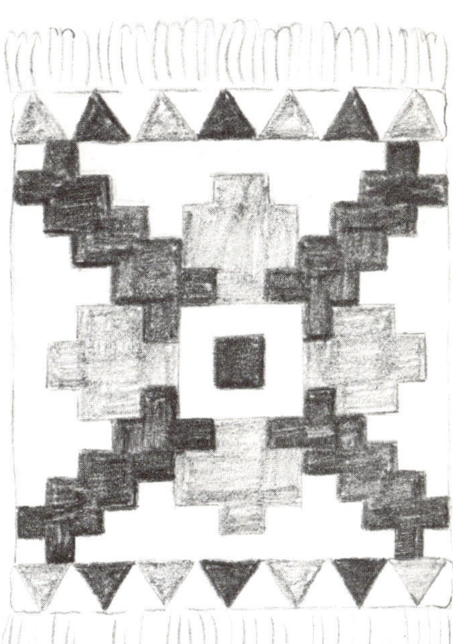

Patterns inspired by natural forms are good for free-hand application on three-dimensional surfaces. These examples were derived from shells, leaves and marks on stones.

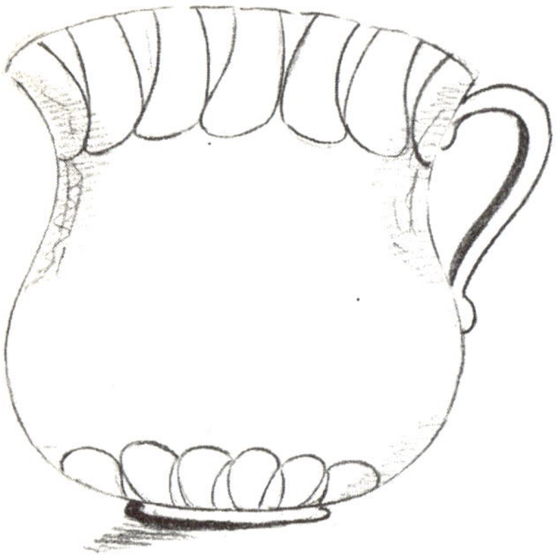

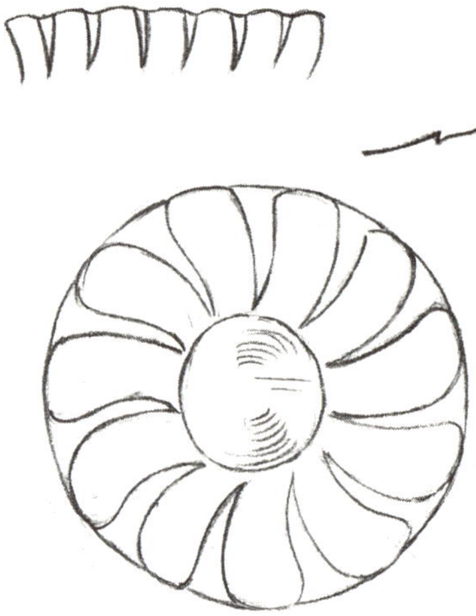

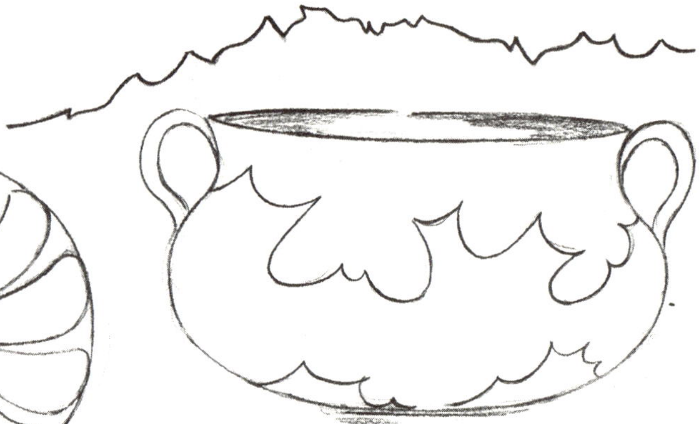

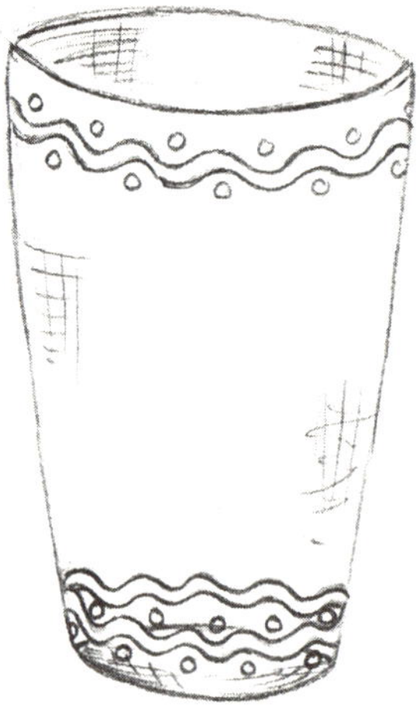

Often a simple line describing or highlighting the shape of an object and following its flow will look better than a complicated pattern. A simple 'doodle' could be very effective. Allow the shape of the object to dictate the design.

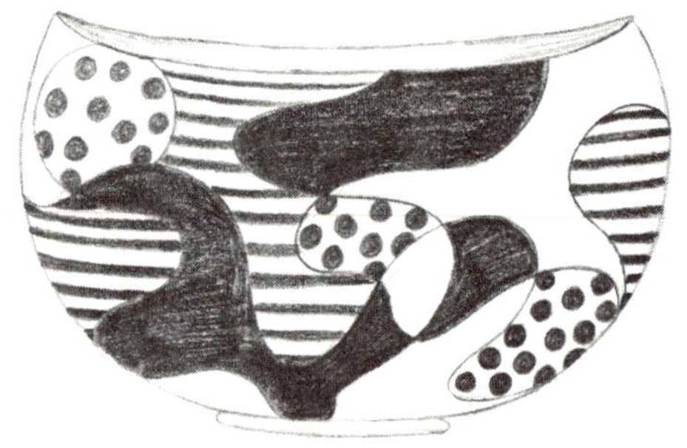

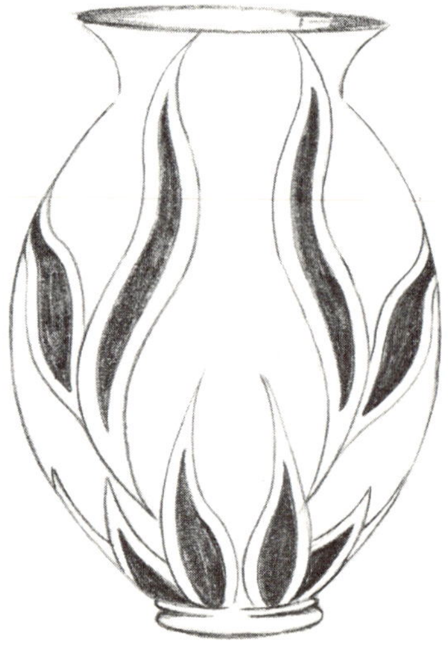

Alternatively, you can apply more formal designs or motifs with a stencil.

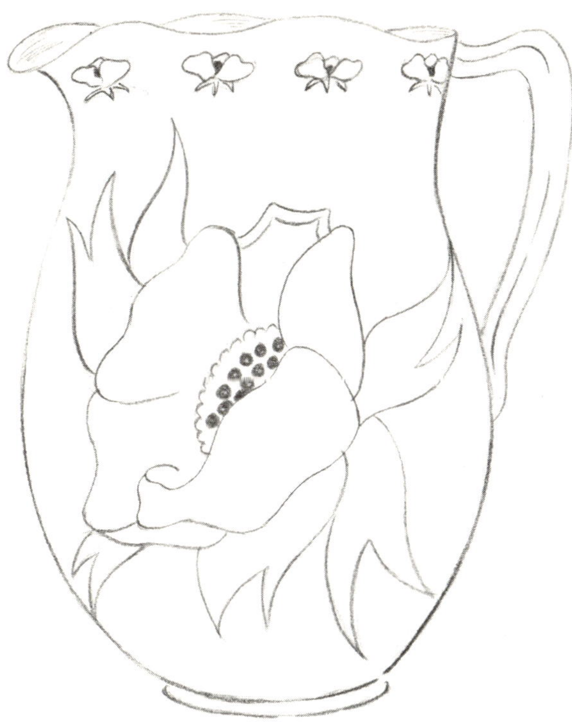

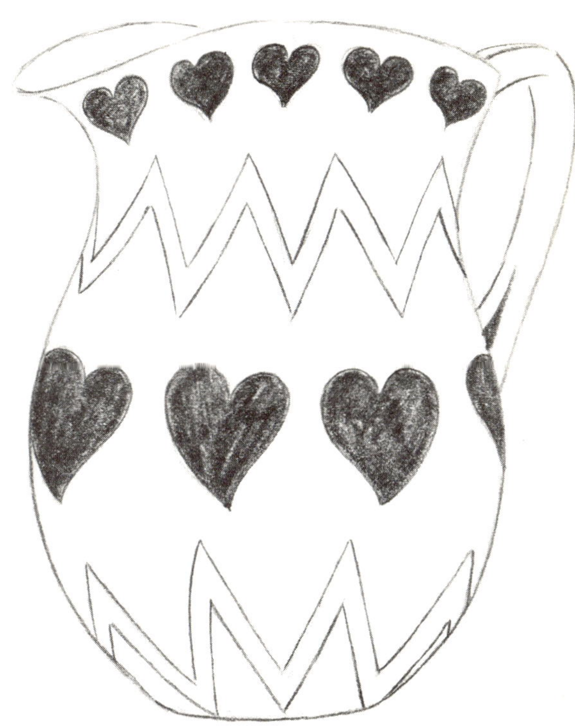

Here are two more examples of patterns applied to pottery, one geometric and one a series of simple marks.

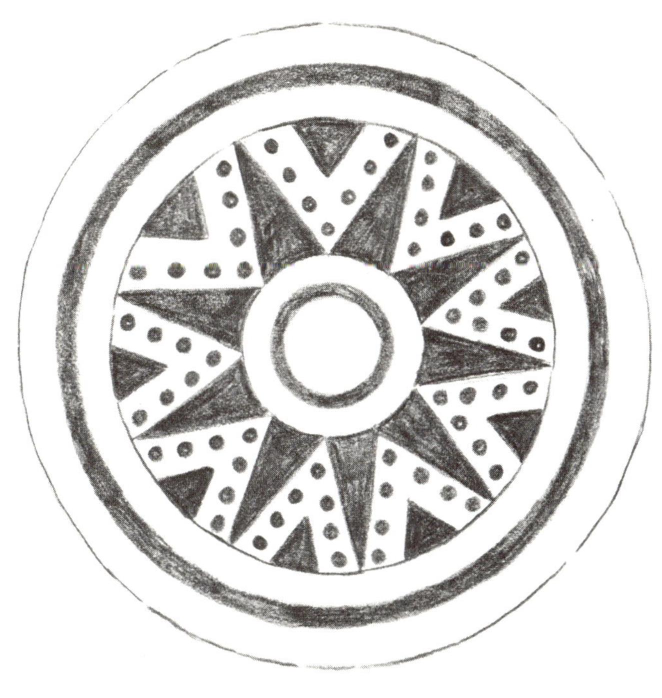

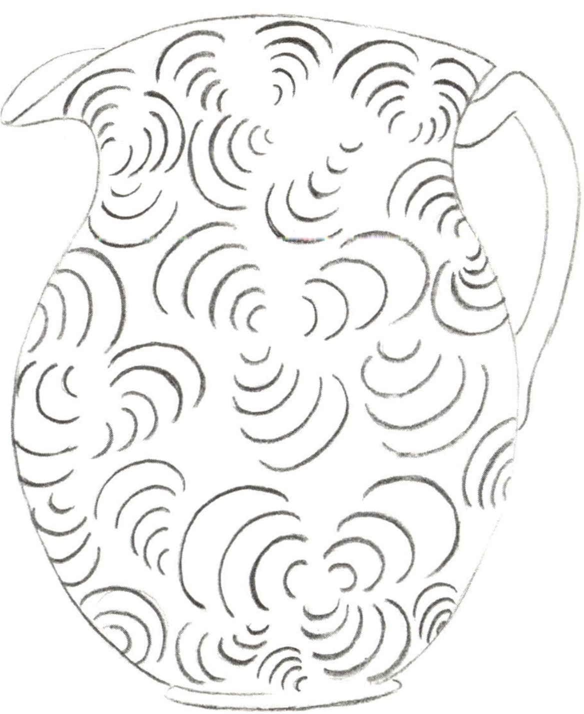

The ideas I have outlined are only a beginning. The possibilities are endless, and once you start to draw patterns you will find that one idea leads to another. Keep a notebook in which to record your ideas and experiments, so that you can refer to it when you want to develop a pattern for a specific purpose. Or make a series of pattern samplers.

This drawing of the design on a silk scarf of the Art Deco period shows an exciting pattern created from ideas similar to some of those I have suggested.

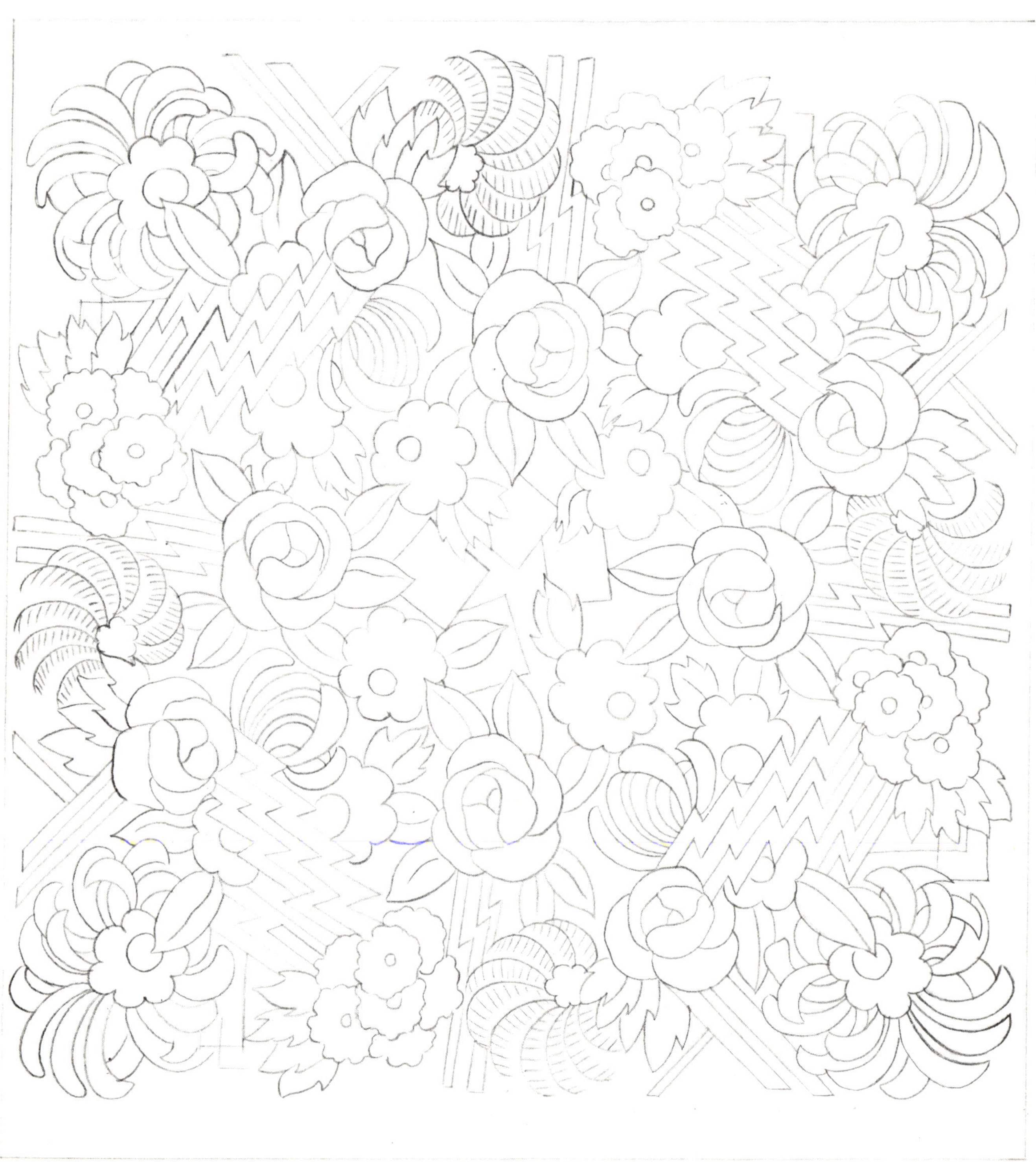